BRICK
22

"All over the world, brick is a catalyzer for progress and building culture development."
Wojciech Czaja

BRICK 22

wienerberger

BRICK 22

Feeling at home

Living together

12 THE COMPETITION
14 EDITORIAL

26 ANNA CYMER
Feeling at Home in Times of Social Distancing

BRICK 22 Category Winner

30 NATURA FUTURA
The House that Inhabits — Productive Urban Housing

38 OYO ARCHITECTS
House DEDE

42 ODDO ARCHITECTS
VH House

46 MCMAHON ARCHITECTURE
Leyton House

50 LANZA ATELIER
Forest House

54 ARHITEKTURA
The Double Brick House

58 USE STUDIO
ABAN House

62 BUREAU SLA AMSTERDAM
House Koopvaardersplantsoen Amsterdam

68 ISABELLA LEBER
Housing Construction in Times of Densification

BRICK 22 Category Winner

72 AVENIER CORNEJO ARCHITECTES
88 housing units + 1 retail space — Rue Danton, Pantin

80 SERGISON BATES ARCHITECTS
Harbour Building Antwerp

84 HILBERINKBOSCH ARCHITECTEN
TV Tube Factory

88 WINGÅRDHS
Basaren

92 DEHULLU ARCHITECTEN
Social Housing: 34 Single-Family Homes in Zwevegem

96 MANGOR & NAGEL
Falkoner Allé 118

100 POWERHOUSE COMPANY
Merckt

104 VERS.A
Mexico

108 WIRTH ARCHITEKTEN
Hulsbergspitze

112 AILTIREACHT ARCHITECTS + DTA – DEREK TYNAN ARCHITECTS
Grattan Court East

116 A2O ARCHITECTEN
Sky One

120 ORANGE ARCHITECTS
Transformation PTT Building

Working together

126 MATEVŽ ČELIK
Office Architecture and Ecology:
Re-assembling Bricks in a New Way

BRICK 22 Category Winner

130 BAUMSCHLAGER EBERLE ARCHITEKTEN
2226 Emmenweid

138 VTN ARCHITECTS
Viettel Academy Educational Center

142 JKMM ARCHITECTS
K-Kampus

146 DIEGO ARRAIGADA ARQUITECTOS
Edificio de Estudios

150 TRANSFORM; PLUSKONTORET ARKITEKTER
Vejen Town Hall

154 HOOBA DESIGN GROUP
Kohan Ceram Central Office Building

158 NERI&HU DESIGN AND RESEARCH OFFICE
The Unified City-Schindler City

162 VIRKKUNEN & CO ARCHITECTS
Imatra Electricity Substation

Sharing public spaces

168 HENRIETTA PALMER
In Search of a Renewed Public Space

BRICK 22 Grand Prize Winner

172 STUDIO ZHU PEI, ARCHITECTURAL DESIGN & RESEARCH INSTITUTE OF TSINGHUA UNIVERSITY
Jingdezhen Imperial Kiln Museum

180 BAROZZI VEIGA
Musée cantonal des Beaux-Arts Lausanne

184 AIA + BB ARQUITECTES + GGG
Camp del Ferro Sports Hall

188 TRANS ARCHITECTUUR STEDENBOUW / V+ BUREAU VERS PLUS DE BIEN-ÊTRE
Leietheater Deinze

192 A+R ARCHITEKTEN
Project Burma Hospital in Myanmar

196 ANTONIO VIRGA ARCHITECTE
Cinema Le Grand Palais

200 COLECTIVO C733
Matamoros Public Market

204 BRENAC & GONZALEZ & ASSOCIÉS
Rosa Parks School

208 MAGÉN ARQUITECTOS
Auditorium-Theatre in the Old Quarter of Illueca

212 B-ARCHITECTEN & BEVK PEROVIĆ ARHITEKTI
Erasmus University College

216 ZERO ENERGY DESIGN LAB ARCHITECTS
Girls' Hostel Block, St. Andrews Institute of Technology

220 UMARCHITEKT, ULRICH MANZ WITH M. KUNTZ AND CH. GATZ
Jewish Museum Franconia

224 DOMINIQUE COULON & ASSOCIÉS
Housing for the Elderly in Huningue

Building outside the box

230 WOJCIECH CZAJA
One Building Block of Many:
A Call to Play and Experiment

BRICK 22 Category Winner

234 NERI&HU DESIGN AND RESEARCH OFFICE
The Brick Wall — Tsingpu Yangzhou Retreat

242 GRAMAZIO KOHLER RESEARCH, ETH ZURICH; INCON.AI; ROB TECHNOLOGIES AG, ZURICH / SWITZERLAND
Augmented Bricklaying

246 BERGER+PARKKINEN ASSOCIATED ARCHITECTS
Paracelsus Bad & Kurhaus

250 WALLMAKERS
Pirouette House

254 BODENSTEINER FEST ARCHITECTS
Casa Rossa Chemnitz

258 BANGKOK PROJECT STUDIO
The Elephant World:
Non-Human-Centered Architecture

262 HARQUITECTES
Clos Pachem Winery

266 CTA | CREATIVE ARCHITECTS
Wall House

270 MONADNOCK & DE ZWARTE HOND
Park Pavilion

BRICK
22

The jury: Brigitte Shim (on screen), Ingrid van der Hejden, Tina Gregorič, Wilfried Kuehn and Jesper Gottlieb

The Competition

For the tenth time, the Brick Award offers international architects an independent platform to present innovative and contemporary brick architecture and make it known to a broad audience around the world.

The aim is not only to find inspiration through extraordinary projects but, above all, to search for new ways and discuss sustainable design concepts to turn visionary architectural approaches into reality with the help of ceramic materials.

This time, 789 buildings from 53 countries were submitted for the award. In a first step, a preliminary jury compiled a shortlist of the 50 most innovative and relevant projects from all submissions. Appointing the preliminary jury according to a rotation system ensures diverse views from people of various countries and cultures, and thus a different perspective for each Brick Award. This year it consisted of the three architecture journalists Anneke Bokern from The Netherlands, Christian Holl from Germany and Andres Kurg from Estonia. These three experts are also responsible for the project texts in this book.

The criteria for the pre-selection have not changed in recent years: the use of ceramic building materials, the degree of innovation, the sustainability of the entire construction process, the architectural quality, and the adequacy of the project, which has been considered since the Brick Award 20, are decisive for a nomination. For the Brick Award 22, however, energy efficiency and the circularity of the building materials served as further important assessment criteria.

In terms of content, the high number and range of submissions indicate a direction which is reflected in the nominations selected by the previous jury: The development of recent years has been continuing and the focus has therefore remained on resource-saving construction. This applies to both technically highly innovative structures, as well as those erected in the traditional way using local materials and craftmanship. Re-use is just as present as the imaginative handling of brick—for example, the use of halved bricks or the use of vertically perforated bricks for ventilation. This almost playful approach leads to concise designs that are remembered. The weighting of the different categories is nearly balanced, which shows that brick is represented in all realms of building typology.

In the second phase of the competition, the winners were determined by a jury of international architects, made up of Jesper Gottlieb from Denmark (winner of the Brick 20 Award for the "City Archive Delft" project), Tina Gregorič from Slovenia, Ingrid van der Heijden from The Netherlands, Wilfried Kuehn from Germany and Brigitte Shim from Canada.

During the selection process, the jurors took into consideration both the cultural context and local traditional building methods as a starting basis for innovative architectural realizations. There was also a consensus on focusing on the concept of well-being for the first time: Would one like to work in this building or spend her/his private time here? The role of this factor in the evaluation was due not least to the issue of COVID-19. That also proved to be the reason why the jury meeting took place as a fixed date in Vienna, as well as online, to involve Brigitte Shim, who was not able to travel to Europe.

This book introduces the 50 nominees, including the winning projects of the Brick Award 22. Each of the buildings is documented with texts, photographs, and plan material. Moreover, the winning projects are also presented in short videos, which can be found at www.brickaward.com.

Dear architecture friends,
We hope you enjoy discovering the trend-setting brick architecture of the Brick Award 22.

BRICK 22

"We treat people and the environment with respect and trust."

Heimo Scheuch
CEO Wienerberger AG

OUR MISSION

"As an innovation leader, we will make an effective contribution for generations with sustainable and smart solutions."

wienerberger

Editorial

Dear architecture enthusiasts,

So far, the third millennium has certainly had more than its fair share of economic and socio-cultural challenges, and although we are still struggling to come to terms with how the COVID-19 pandemic has impacted our lives, that is no excuse to forget the burning challenge of our age, climate change.

Crises are often regarded as crossroads where we make decisions that will determine the future. At the same time, they can be seen as opportunities to be seized. Oftentimes, they radically accelerate long overdue social and political changes. And in retrospect, crises can in fact turn out to have been phases of focused problem solving. Viewed in this light, architecture often acts as a mirror of its time.

During the COVID-19 pandemic, our homes have taken on new roles, serving as makeshift offices and schools. Simultaneously, the trend towards bigger homes and the new urban exodus are taking a toll on the environment: urban densification continues unabated, while at the same time previously untouched countryside is developed and green spaces are concreted over.

As a leading international supplier of smart building materials and infrastructure solutions, Wienerberger wants to make a substantial contribution to tackling these key challenges with a sustainability concept based on three core environmental themes: decarbonization, circular economy and biodiversity. The products and system solutions developed by the company offer architects and builders effective tools for residential and commercial construction, with the goal of improving people's quality of life, protecting the environment and revolutionizing how we build in the future.

Once again, the architectural responses to these challenges that were entered for the Tenth Brick Award are as exceptional as they are innovative. Built of brick, they are also solid, energy-efficient and sustainable. In a nutshell, they have all the qualities that are essential if we are to manage the consequences of climate change and ensure that future generations have the same opportunities as we do today.

We are proud that the Tenth Brick Award offers these outstanding architectural works a stage where their aesthetic quality, form and design can be shown the appreciation they deserve. We would like to thank the international jury of architects who selected the winners of the Brick Award for their valuable contributions in the selection process, and of course all those who submitted their projects.

We hope that as connoisseurs of architecture you will enjoy reading this BRICK 22 book and find inspiration and pleasure as you explore these remarkable architectural projects.

Heimo Scheuch
CEO Wienerberger AG

Feeling at home
Living together
Working together
Sharing public spaces
Building outside the box

Feeling at home

26	ANNA CYMER **Feeling at Home in Times of Social Distancing**	50	LANZA ATELIER **Forest House**
30	NATURA FUTURA **The House that Inhabits — Productive Urban Housing**	54	ARHITEKTURA **The Double Brick House**
38	OYO ARCHITECTS **House DEDE**	58	USE STUDIO **ABAN House**
42	ODDO ARCHITECTS **VH House**	62	BUREAU SLA AMSTERDAM **House Koopvaardersplantsoen Amsterdam**
46	MCMAHON ARCHITECTURE **Leyton House**		

BRICK 22 Category Winner

ANNA CYMER
Feeling at Home in Times of Social Distancing

Anna Cymer

We probably should be getting used to more and more surprising and dramatic events. The climate crisis is causing unpredictable changes and everything indicates that they will increase. How shall environmental challenges and the experience of the pandemic alter our way of living?

The climate crisis and the pandemic have changed our thinking about architecture. The whole world is wondering: Do we really need all these office buildings and skyscrapers? We appreciated public spaces, we saw the advantages of 15-minute city, we are still looking for more environmentally-friendly materials and building technologies. But probably one of the most important questions of our era is: How should we build our houses if we want to feel comfortable and stay safe in an increasingly unpredictable environment?

Two years ago, any discussion about architecture seemed fixed. We more or less knew what to do to make cities better places to live, to build in a more sustainable, greener, eco-friendlier, etc., manner. The worldwide pandemic has turned everything upside down. Just like we forgot how bad disposable tableware and other single-use items are for the environment, we likewise returned to idealizing single-family houses as the safest places to live when contact with other people can be dangerous and even a small private garden is priceless.

This makes debate about architecture in the 21st century more complicated. The climate crisis is forcing us to build less and more densely, to live in houses with a smaller usable area and more neighbors around. But how can living in multi-family houses in densely-built estates be promoted in the face of the pandemic and the necessity for social distancing? Have we reached a deadlock?

Talking about single-family houses is difficult, since we have realized that architecture places a great burden on our environment and that we should make considerable changes in our way of building to reduce the impact of climate change. Single-family housing is the least sustainable and environmentally friendly, "selfish," energy-eating type of residential construction. It is often bigger than needed, built at the expense of trees and greenery, fenced in and isolated, and forces us to use private cars. At the same time, however, living in a house with a garden is one of the primary human needs, especially in this modern age of intense urbanization. It is the most desired way of living in the western world, as well as the most popular one on a global scale.

There is no single, good answer for what to do in the face of these dilemmas. It is impossible for everyone to live in single-family housing, as well as to forbid this type of living. For our tired and exhausted planet, it would be better not to build oversized single-family houses, but we know there will be more of them. Perhaps one of best methods to promote a sustainable, environmentally-respectful, energy-efficient way of building single-family houses is to show and appreciate good projects.

Among all building materials, brick fits perfectly to modern architecture for families. Brick is traditional, evokes good memories, and is associated with warmth and safety. At the same time, brick allows even very modern shapes to be built. Brick is natural, recyclable and easy to rebuild or remodel with. Recycled brick is not only better for environment, but also fashionable—there are many architects who intentionally utilize the features of this material, its patina, texture, color and "imperfection."

Even if we regard single-family housing as bad and no longer relevant to the way of living in our era, we cannot ignore the fact that a house should be healthy and safe. And again, brick is the kind of material that fulfills these conditions without any additional devices or installations, which makes it easier to use and more energy-effective.

When observing trends in housing architecture, one notices a few main ideas which are similar in many countries. One is related to the greenery on the plot: Many houses are very carefully constructed to fit in with the trees. Cutting them down is beyond any architect's fantasy or private builder's vision: The house simply takes on the shape of the open space between the trees, becoming a background for them, like part of a theater scene where plants are the main actors. Nature takes front stage rather than the architect's or client's ego.

Another group of houses designed in this new way of architectural thinking are being constructed in the cities. Here we can find numerous simple blocks connected to the urban fabric. Often they are ascetic, plain structures designed to blend in with the urban space, to merge with neighboring houses. Architects are trying to fill the gaps in the streets, to create dense and coherent neighborhoods. Sometimes it can be done by mimicry, imitation, or by maximum simplicity, but sometimes by contrast. This way of completing an urban landscape is especially interesting, since it often happens in relation with the past, with historical styles, the character or spirit of the district. Brick is easy to combine with other building materials, which makes the process of composing brick buildings together with the surroundings more creative and varied.

We must face the challenges that are changing our world, otherwise our future will be terrible. Architecture is one of the fields where changes are needed. It has been said that the most sustainable buildings are those already built. Every new structure means another strain on the planet. We will not stop building, but we can and should look for shapes, materials, models and forms that are as comfortable for us as they are for the environment.

NATURA FUTURA
The House that Inhabits — Productive Urban Housing

José Fernando Gomez

ARCHITECT/S
Natura Futura, Babahoyo/Ecuador

LOCATION
Babahoyo, Ecuador

BUILDING PURPOSE
Housing, education, workshop

CONSTRUCTION PERIOD
2020

BRICK TYPE
Clay blocks, facing bricks, roof tiles, paving bricks

BRICK
22 Category Winner

The "La Casa que Habita" project is a statement, indeed a manifesto, for the Natura Futura architecture collective. Not just one against the commercialization of the city, which is pushing many people to the edge and tearing the stimulating mix of work, production and living apart. But one that also gives the brick a symbolic function as a building material by making it appear formative. As a traditional building material, it is often associated with poorer sections of the population, too often hidden, plastered, or painted over. Here, the architects are determined to demonstrate and further explore its value for a lively, habitable city.

The structure ties in with the traditional house type of the Latin American city, which is still characteristic in many cases in Babahoyo, and takes full advantage of the thirty meters that the twelve-meter-wide property extends downwards: Commercial space can be found on the ground floor; an apartment, as well as five rooms of an educational institution lie above it on the protruding upper floor. Skylights on the ridge and a narrow corridor along the outer walls provide light. Wood, another material considered to be for those less well-off, was used and valued for the roof construction. It is left visible and integrated into the stairwell railing. A narrow balcony, fully glazed and assigned to the apartment, lines the entire width of the upper floor. Shutters can be closed so that the balcony is shaded, yet remains usable.

Bricks are employed in a variety of ways in this project and differentiated in their sizes to make the various uses legible as well: The partition walls are laid in the stretcher bond, reinforced on the outer façades, and feature continuous joints, as well as clinker bricks in the parapet area. The rough, irregular structure on the walls creates a lively surface, especially when the sunrays fall on them as glancing light.

> "We see the brick as an instrument of incidence, transgression and transformation."

The sidewalk and a seat in front of the house are likewise made of bricks. Here the ratio of the "poorer" materials to others is reversed — also on the surfaces of the few places where the underflooring and construction consist of other building materials.

Through the compact combination of usages and the opening of the living area towards the street space, that very density of life which Natura Futura sees as threatened is established. The warmth of the wood and brick surfaces generates an atmosphere of immediacy that facilitates the individual appropriation. [ch]

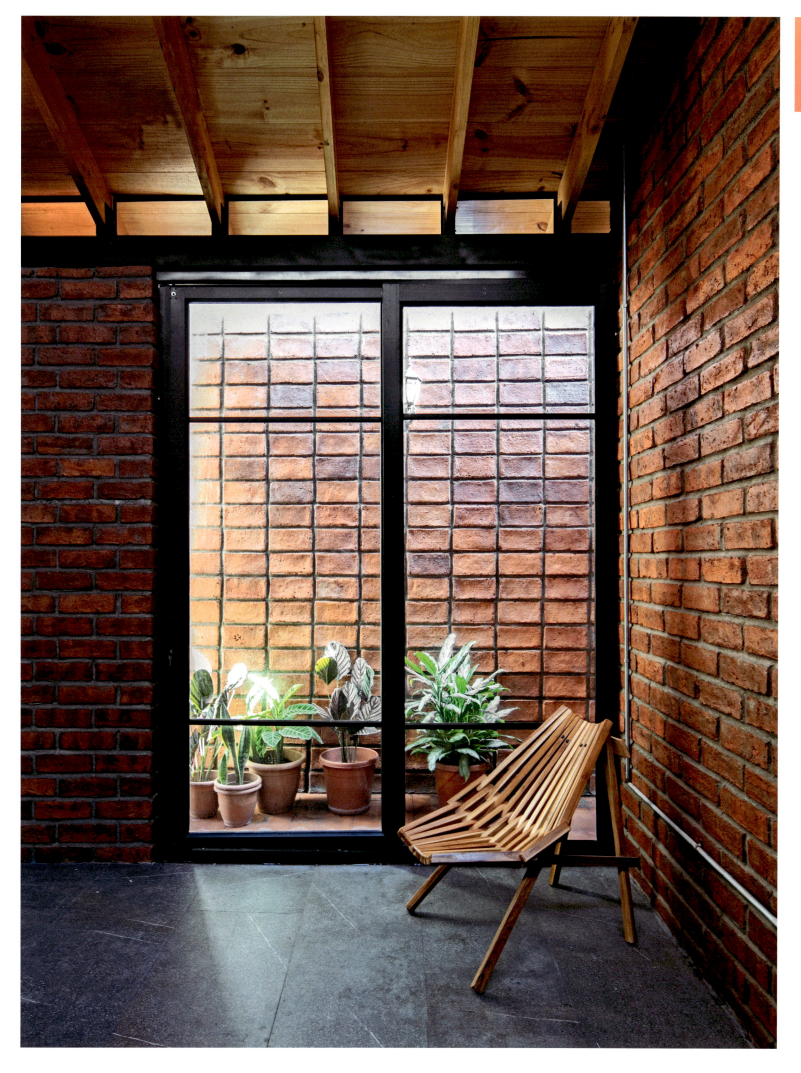

The House that Inhabits — Productive Urban Housing

The brick confidently presents itself as a modern, high-quality building material.

Shared kitchen upstairs

The House that Inhabits — Productive Urban Housing

Jury Statement

"The boundaries of this project lie far beyond the building envelope. It speaks of small-scale initiatives that stretch the typology of mixed-use buildings and, by doing so, make a positive contribution to the quality of urban life in the contemporary city center. In combination with the unusual spatial organization and materialization, it makes the La Casa que Habita a true manifesto.

Spatially, the building blends into its surroundings in a refined way. The whole exudes tranquility and restraint. The architects have managed to make maximum use of the plot in a clever way. The spatial quality is determined by the relationship between the consistently implemented brick, the detailing and the ubiquitous daylight. The three long strips of light cultivate flexibility and bring poetry. The jury thinks of the project as a happy place."

The House that Inhabits — Productive Urban Housing

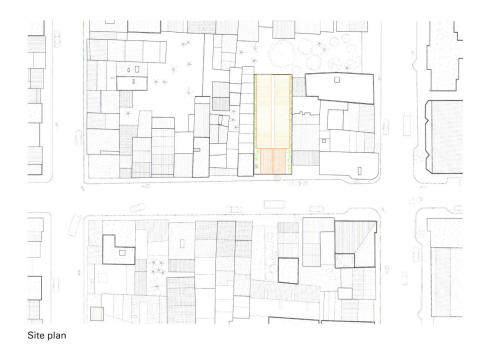

Site plan

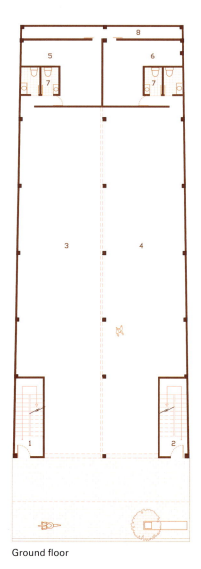

Ground floor

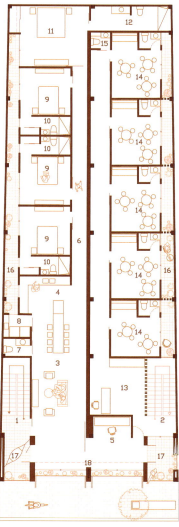

First floor

Several filters separate the interior of the upper floor from the outside space.

OYO ARCHITECTS
House DEDE

Nigel Jooren and Xander Denduyver

ARCHITECT/S
OYO Architects,
Ghent/Belgium

LOCATION
Drongen, Belgium

BUILDING PURPOSE
Single-family housing

CONSTRUCTION PERIOD
2018–2019

BRICK TYPE
Facing bricks

House DEDE is in Drongen, a suburb of Ghent. The private builders—a family with three children—had consciously decided for a plot of land on which only a relatively small building volume could be realized, because they wanted to have as large a garden as possible. An old brick barn still stood on the property, but its volume, according to the development plan, could only be doubled at most.

> "One of the first material use decisions was to recycle the bricks from the derelict barn for both sustainable and aesthetic purposes."

Consequently, the barn was torn down. Except for the gable roof, its cubature was retained in the new building volume, but was quite literally "crossed" with an additional structure: a second, single-story transverse bar slides through the elongated, two-story barn volume at a 45-degree angle. This created further spaces with a three-sided garden view, but also intimate outdoor areas around the house.

The house faces the street with a largely closed façade, only interrupted by a window on the upper floor shielded by a brick grille. Hidden behind the closed concrete wall on the ground floor is a storage room with a bicycle garage. A footpath runs past it on the left to the main entrance, which leads into the new transverse wing. To the left of the entrance, one reaches the study, to the right, the open kitchen and the dining area behind it. The kitchen is situated exactly at the intersection of the two wings. Opening in front of it is the living area, which features a striking wooden spiral staircase. It winds through a round hole in the exposed concrete ceiling to the upper floor, where the bathroom and the master bedroom are located on the garden side. At the other end there is a sequence of three children's rooms, which can be joined together using sliding doors to form a large playroom.

On the ground floor, exposed concrete with formwork patterns determines the appearance both inside and outside. All rooms open to the garden through floor-to-ceiling windows. The façades of the upper floor, on the other hand, were made from the reused bricks of the old barn. The mortar was not scraped off, but oozes out of the joints, lending the façades a pronounced relief effect.

The guiding principle behind the design was to anchor the house in its location. This happens, on the one hand, through the intensive interaction between the interior and exterior space, which arises from the cross shape of the volume and the large window areas. However, the adoption of the cubature of the old barn and, above all, the reused bricks mean that the single-family house captures the spirit of the place and enables it to live on in an abstract form. [ab]

House DEDE

The cubature of the old brick barn was supplemented by an inserted volume.

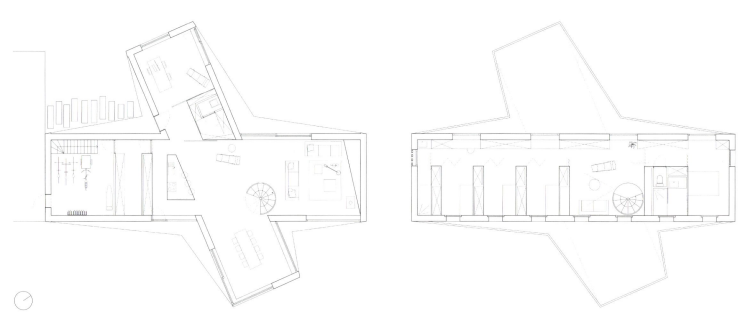

Ground floor

First floor

Funnel-like entrance situation

Inside as well, the interleaving creates exciting spatial situations.

ODDO ARCHITECTS
VH House

Marek Obtulovic, Mai Lan Chi Obtulovicova and Nguyen Duc Trung

ARCHITECT/S
ODDO Architects, Hanoi/Vietnam

LOCATION
Hanoi, Vietnam

BUILDING PURPOSE
Single-family housing

CONSTRUCTION PERIOD
2018

BRICK TYPE
Clay blocks, facings bricks, paving bricks

From above, the picture of the Hanoi district in which the VH House is located shows a dense development of houses of varying heights, the roofs of which are crowned by attached huts as extensions. ODDO Architects have taken up and transformed this informal principle — and thus created a microcosm of apartment and open space, visual connections, communal and retreat areas out of a simple, small house. At the same time, they have drawn upon a traditional typology of long, narrow, three-sided buildings with only one façade. This type of house with courtyards inside for lighting and ventilation is a reaction to the fact that property prices correlate with the width of the house: Only a narrow façade ensures reasonably affordable prices.

"A light-filled house with gardens wrapped in a porous brick façade."

The building parcel for the family of four measures 4.1 by 16 meters. Part of a densely built-up structure, it offers some space at both ends to the next house wall and is bordered on the northern long side by a small open space through which the house can be entered. On the two front sides of the house, narrow, green buffer zones with an open brick wall are placed as light wells, allowing the full-surface glazing behind them to provide sufficient light. The house is designed like a white box, open at the top, on which three brick cubes are placed at a distance from one another. This also took the tight budget into consideration — bricks and their processing are cheap here. The ground floor is covered with glass between the three brick boxes, so that three distinct areas are also defined on the ground floor, even if the living room and kitchen with dining area merge and the children's bedroom can be opened with a sliding door to ventilate the house along its entire length. The two outer cubes are separated from the ground floor by a glass joint, which provides additional light and does not make the attachments appear too heavy on the inside; the middle cube is slightly raised for this purpose, but this can only be seen from the outside if one looks very closely.

Proceeding from east to west, the three boxes become more and more open. The back one, the bedroom, is still executed as a closed space, but its walls are laid with every second brick protruding slightly. This corresponds with the second cube, which, as a small, closed courtyard with a round opening, is no longer covered and was laid with gaps in its upper half. Finally, the third cube is fully open: Its walls are just high enough to serve as the parapet of a small, leafy terrace. All three are green: the eastern one with plants hanging down from the roof, the other two as small gardens. The glass joints also influence the atmosphere inside, which appears open and friendly despite the cramped conditions. [ch]

VH House

Western terrace

The distances between the brick cubes result in airy zoning.

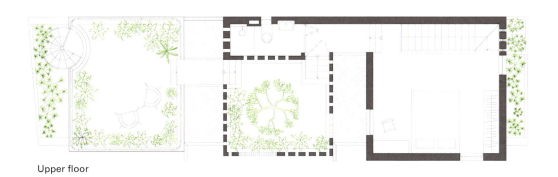

Upper floor

Ground floor

MCMAHON ARCHITECTURE
Leyton House

Louise and Sean McMahon

ARCHITECT/S
McMahon Architecture, London / Great Britain

LOCATION
London, Great Britain

BUILDING PURPOSE
Single-family housing

CONSTRUCTION PERIOD
2018–2020

BRICK TYPE
Facing bricks

This end-of-terrace house, erected in the northwest of the City of London, shows how a spacious apartment can be created with imagination and a good feel for the material, even on a small plot of land. The area in which it stands is marked by a row house development typical of London, which at this point changes from one that accompanies the street to one lined up in the depths of the property. The lot on which Leyton House was built is the first in this sequence, which explains why it is longitudinally to the street and has a side entrance.

A brick wall featuring a lattice structure where windows are behind it ensures the privacy of the living area parallel to the street, as well as the open spaces on both sides of the house. To be able to offer sufficient living space, the building has a basement along the entire length of the small, narrow property and thus has three full floors. A light well on one side, an atrium on the other and a floor plan that brings together those functions requiring little light in the middle ensure that there are easily usable spaces in the basement, too. Above this, the building is visually divided into two parts: Compared to the massive ground floor, which is characterized by brickwork, the upper floor is designed as a lightweight wooden structure with a bright wooden façade, which lends the house a somewhat pavilion-like quality and disguises its true size. An accentuated chimney creates a vertical antithesis to the otherwise horizontally structured composition. The upper story is offset from the ground floor so that a skylight on the street side provides additional light. In contrast to the windows facing the street, the large-sized glazing oriented to the side opens the view to the surroundings.

> "Leyton House is defined by its material integrity and use of brick."

On the ground floor, a brick was chosen for the walls bordering the outdoor areas as well as for the house walls, the color variations of which range from a light, watery pink to orange to the typical brick red. The rough and irregularly structured surface creates a liveliness that harmonizes well with the wooden surfaces of the ceiling construction and unobtrusively contrasts the windows framed by wooden reveals, as well as the concrete details of the interior construction. The finely balanced interplay of different materials is rounded off by clay plaster walls in pastel shades on the upper and lower floors, as well as brightly glazed Siberian larch on the upper floor, but the sophisticated material concept also develops an enriching effect towards the street area. [ch]

Leyton House

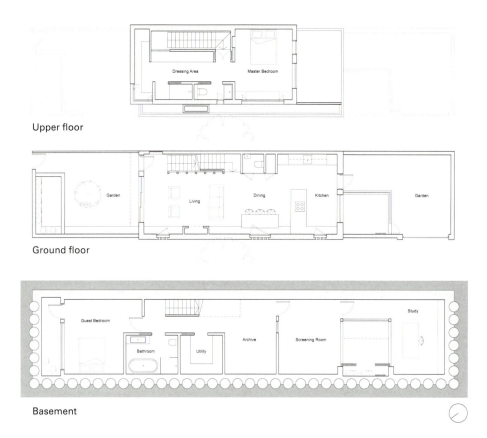

Upper floor

Ground floor

Basement

View into the garden

Basement

LANZA ATELIER
Forest House

Isabel Abascal and Alessandro Arienzo

ARCHITECT/S
LANZA Atelier, Mexico City / Mexico

LOCATION
Ocoyoacac, Mexico

BUILDING PURPOSE
Single-family housing

CONSTRUCTION PERIOD
2017–2020

BRICK TYPE
Clay blocks, facing bricks, paving bricks

Located on the edge of a pine grove, close to a highway, and not far from Mexico City, the Forest House hides its character from the approaching visitors. Its façade is a long, one-story brick wall, curving slightly towards the entrance that is lifted a few steps higher from the street level. The handmade stone in light terracotta hues, ranging from yellow to pink, dominates the whole building and garden, continuing in the interior, finishing the rectangular rooms and the undulating wall that ties the diverse parts of the house into one whole. From the plan, this combination of a continuous, animate line of the enclosing wall and the right angles of the rooms could be compared to a cubist composition. The experience of the visitor, however, comes closer to following a "promenade architecturale," where the movement through the different areas of the house and garden offers carefully framed views to the surrounding nature and provides a play of light flooding in from the openings in the curving concrete roof, and shadows cast by the separating lattice brickwork wall.

> "Carefully cut handmade bricks seemed to become flexible in the hands of the brick masons."

The program of this 600-square-meter-large house includes two buildings: a one-story house for the family with two kids and a spacious two-story guesthouse, connected by the curving wall and opening to a common garden area. The bedrooms and the corridor in the family house have roof windows for morning light; the living room and dining area are turned towards the east and connected to the garden space through large French doors. The detailing is minimal and carefully selected: The natural surfaces of the yellowish stone and gray concrete are supported by the pale green metal surfaces of the window frames and the spiral staircase to the basement, and the warm finishing of the oak wood furniture. The house was composed taking into account the pre-existing pine trees, and its program is turned towards the enclosed garden space, closing itself off from the noise of the road. In several places, the rectangular bricks had to be manually cut by bricklayers to build the curves of the walls which adapt themselves to the trees and fit infrastructure inside their non-standard structures. Leftovers from this work, producing many unusual ceramic forms, were arranged by the architects into wall pictures.

The Forest House was designed by architects Isabel Abascal and Alessandro Arienzo from the Atelier Lanza. The sculptural concrete roof surfaces and the undulating walls following natural traces speak of their interest in mid-20th century modernist heritage in Latin America, dominated by world-famous architects like Lina Bo Bardi, Oscar Niemeyer and Luis Barragán. But in particular, the architects point to their attraction towards the recently rediscovered work of the Cuban Ricardo Porro, whose National Art School in Havana (together with Vittorio Garatti and Roberto Gottardi) from the early 1960s is a landmark building in its creative use of brick and in combining local traditions with structural inventiveness. [ak]

Forest House

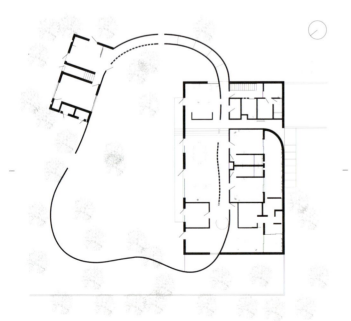

Ground floor

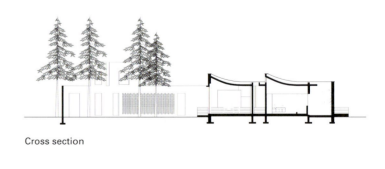

Cross section

The rectangular spaces are also characterized by the rounded wall and roof shapes.

ARHITEKTURA
The Double Brick House

Boštjan Gabrijelčič   Aleš and Peter Gabrijelčič

ARCHITECT/S
ARHITEKTURA,
Ljubljana / Slovenia

LOCATION
Ljubljana, Slovenia

BUILDING PURPOSE
Two-family house

CONSTRUCTION PERIOD
2016–2020

BRICK TYPE
Brick veneer

The Double Brick House stands in the Rožna Dolina neighborhood in Ljubljana, amidst a mixed and typologically diverse suburban development. Nearby there are spacious villas from the early 20th century, standard apartment blocks from the Socialist era, and single-family homes from the 1990s, where the building has stopped halfway and the gray insulation panels still dominate the façades. In this context, the laconic black box of the Double Brick House is almost like a conceptual object that negates its surroundings by not copying its forms, but at the same time aspires to bring order to this heterogeneous context.

Built on a narrow plot that is pressed between its older neighbors, the three-story house is six meters wide and 30 meters long. It is a home for two families, both with an almost identical living unit of 170 square meters. One has their entrance from the street, the other one from the side. Both homes have single-space living rooms and kitchens on the ground floor, children's bedrooms on the first floor and master bedrooms with adjacent terraces on the second. The architects from the Slovenian office Arhitektura have described their principle as that of subtraction: The building was conceived as a monolith that has been gradually modified by removing functionally superfluous volumes. The result is a minimalist design with carefully selected materials and details. Already the street front with its vertical wooden finishing, an almost invisible entrance door on the ground floor level and dark brick surface on the upper levels shows a provocative reversal of the standard logic in architecture. Nor is the functional sequence of spaces directly readable from the street. The visual legibility of the structure is further complicated by the sequence of vertical windows on the side elevations on the first-floor level, indicating narrow children's bedrooms behind each window.

> "The architectural approach was to make the two properties appear as a single structure, united by dark gray-brown brickwork and larch wood window frames and door reveals."

Contrary to the dark brown brick façades of the exterior, the white interiors speak of light and air and the rectangular, undivided windows provide framed views to the visual mix of the surroundings. Yet, rather than being an inward-looking capsule cut off from its social settings, the architects hope that the house would be a starting point for further changes in the area. Their desire is that through negotiations and dialogue, the neighbors would follow the example of the house, but not so much its aesthetics as its care for details and materials: "Using underground conduction of electrical conductors, repairing the sidewalks, fixing roads, mending fences and revamping green gardens." This is a brave idea and an admirable way to extend the program of formal minimalism to meet its real-life circumstances. [ak]

The Double Brick House

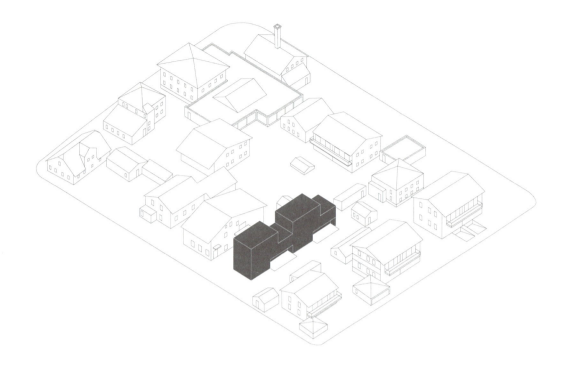

A volume that mediates between the different scales in the area through its structuring.

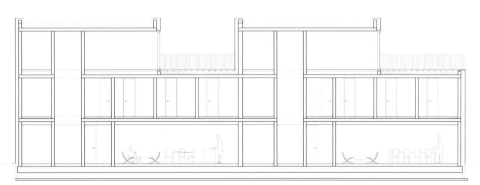

Longitudinal section

USE STUDIO
ABAN House

Mina Moeinoddini and Mohammad Arab

ARCHITECT/S
USE Studio, Isfahan/Iran

LOCATION
Isfahan, Iran

BUILDING PURPOSE
Single-family housing

CONSTRUCTION PERIOD
2016–2018

BRICK TYPE
Clay blocks, handmade bricks made in traditional kilns around Isfahan

Aban House is an all-brick, single-family home, located in the old part of Isfahan, not far from the 17th century Naqsh-e Jahan Square and the Shah Mosque that are major landmarks on the UNESCO World Heritage list. The historic fabric of the area is woven with narrow and twisted streets and residential structures from the 19th and early 20th century. Behind their discreet street fronts, these inward-turned houses are organized around central courtyards with rich ornamentation, arcades that provide shade from sunlight, and central pools of water. This typology has been one of the inspiration points for the architects Mina Moeinoddini and Mohammad Arab from USE Studio, in the house they designed as their own home. Their aim was also to restore residential function to this historic neighborhood, which had been neglected in recent decades. The characteristic dichotomies of historic Isfahan houses—light and shadow, mass and voids, introversion and extroversion—have been transpositioned here in a way that allows exciting spatial solutions and caters for the needs of contemporary life.

The house is built on a narrow, trapezoidal, 250-square-meter site that is seven meters wide at the entrance side and thirty meters long. Using an ancient Iranian geometry of 3×3 modules, the architects have split the traditional courtyard into three interconnected yards and shifted them off the center. On the ground floor, a spacious salon next to the entrance opens to the garden in front of the house; on the same floor the library and the guest room share a courtyard in the back corner of the site. One floor above, the family room opens to a courtyard at the back, with views to the lower level, and their daughter Aban's room opens to the yard in front, a "joy space" as the architects have called it. The yards adjacent to the rooms function as light shafts that connect different levels and spaces in unexpected ways, and at the same time extend the spaces, undoing the rigid inside-outside borders of the house. On the top floor roof terrace, the introspective character of the house is turned around. Superb views open from there to the surroundings, with the turquoise dome of the Shah Mosque, courtyards of the neighboring historic houses, and occasional trees sticking out from among the sandstone-colored built structures.

"Back to basics, out of the box."

The yellow sandstone brick used for the Aban House has been a traditional building material in central Iran for centuries. In the dry and hot weather with more than twenty degrees of variation in diurnal temperature, it maintains a balanced indoor climate. It also has been a material for ornamentation in private and public architecture. In the Aban House the brick is employed in a minimalist tradition, combining abstract masses in a sculptural way and finishing the surfaces with maximum care for detail. Its surfaces provide background for the bright, natural sunlight and sharp shadows cast on the walls and patios, and greenery planted on the terraces. As a house that is also the architects' own home, Aban House belongs to a series of buildings where experimentation and the study of forms interpenetrates with daily life and its needs. Once-abstract concepts are put to a test here and are allowed to intervene more openly in life practices; to invent new forms for living together. [ak]

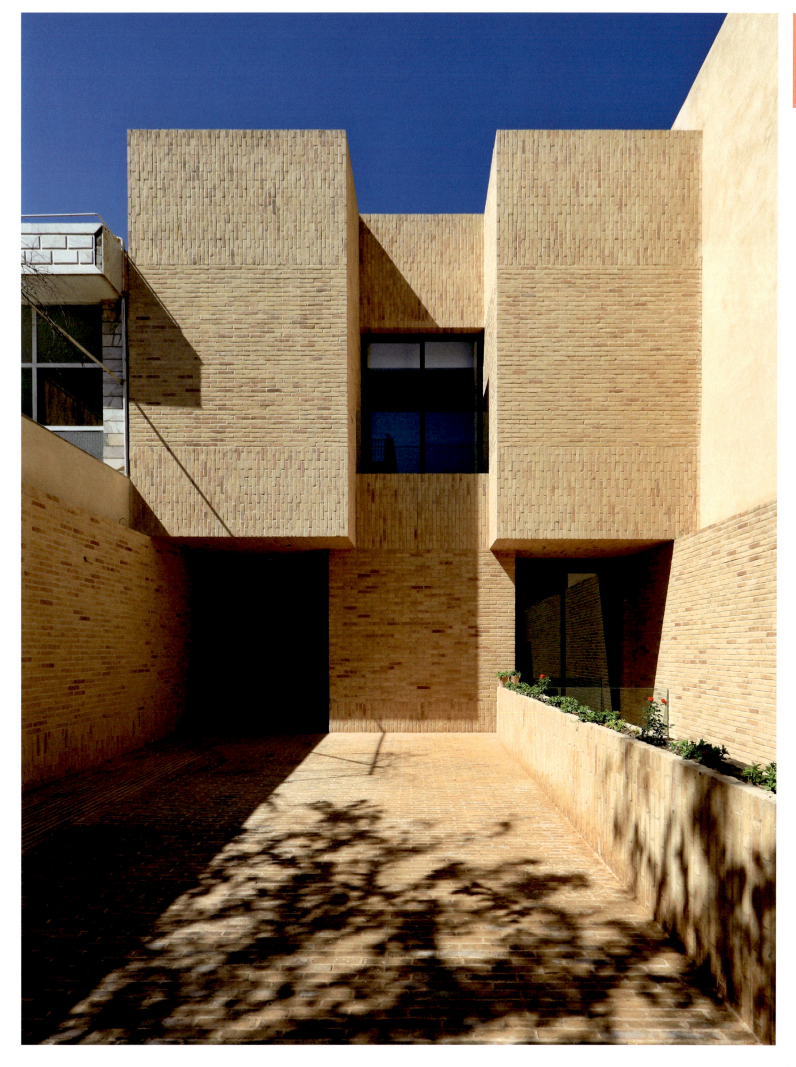

ABAN House

The house is woven into the urban structure.

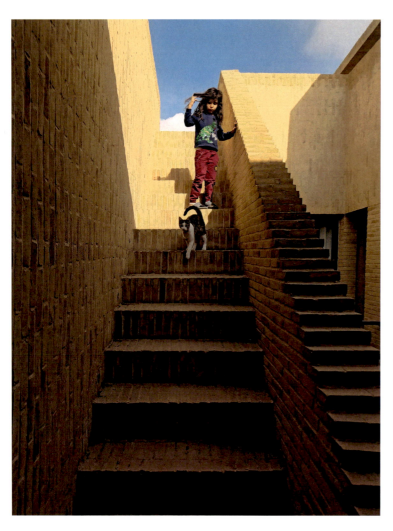

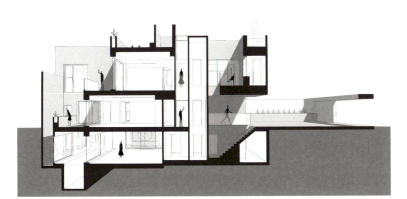
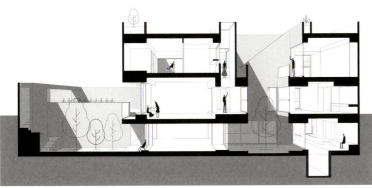

Cutaway views

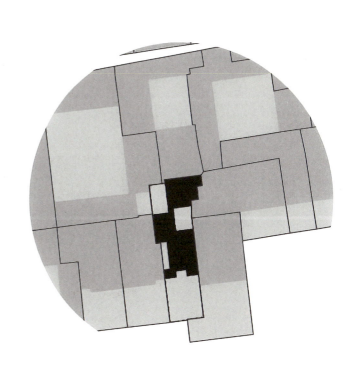

Site plan

BUREAU SLA AMSTERDAM
House Koopvaardersplantsoen Amsterdam

Peter van Assche and Ninja Zurheide

ARCHITECT/S
Bureau SLA, Amsterdam / The Netherlands

LOCATION
Amsterdam, The Netherlands

BUILDING PURPOSE
Single-family housing

CONSTRUCTION PERIOD
2017–2019

BRICK TYPE
Facing bricks

No ordinary Dutch end-of-terrace structure, the house at Koopvaardersplantsoen sees itself as a built manifesto against the industrialized construction industry. In the Netherlands, the construction process usually follows the same linear course from client to architect to general contractor to subcontractor. All of them play a fixed role in the process and do not think outside the box. As Bureau SLA discovered, a lot of information is lost along the way and errors are therefore committed. That is why the architects declared the house in Amsterdam to be a test object. They acted as client, planner, and general contractor in personal union when realizing it. Curious about whether the result would be more architectural and living quality, they also wanted to learn from the craftsmen who carried out the work.

> "Leftover bricks and innovative jointing give new design looks."

At first glance, the result is a classic brick row house with a flat roof that offers 160 square meters of living space on four floors. Inside there are partly five-meter-high rooms, a split level and a mezzanine floor, which means that there are visual connections between the different levels. The kitchen and a separately accessible work room are situated on the ground floor. Distributed over several levels above are the living and sleeping floors. A walled garden serves as an outdoor space.

Since the architects were in control of the entire project, they were able to execute several special requests. Together with the plasterer, they developed an intentionally imperfect plaster and had the specially made window frames installed behind the masonry. The design of the brick façades is also unusual: They consist of various leftovers that had been sorted out in the factory due to color and production errors. To assure that the mixture of the very different brick types still forms a unit, mortar slurry was coated over the masonry and rubbed off irregularly. This technique had formerly been used on farmhouses in the Netherlands. But there are also some architectural models, including the St. Benediktusberg Abbey in Vaals by Dom Hans van der Laan and the Galeriehaus am Kupfergraben in Berlin by David Chipperfield. In both cases, however, the slurry is applied so thickly and evenly that the brick is barely visible. In Amsterdam, on the other hand, they opted for a thin slurry of quartz sand, air-hardening lime, clay powder and white cement — a secret recipe developed by a master joint filler. As incidental as the mortar layer looks at first glance, it was applied with care. So, what did the architects learn? According to their own statement, they now understand better why a general contractor sometimes says that something is not possible when he actually thinks it is complex. They developed a better understanding of the construction processes and therefore more self-confidence in the design. And they constructed a row house with an unexpected spatial effect that is tailored entirely to personal wishes. However, building this house was not faster or cheaper. [ab]

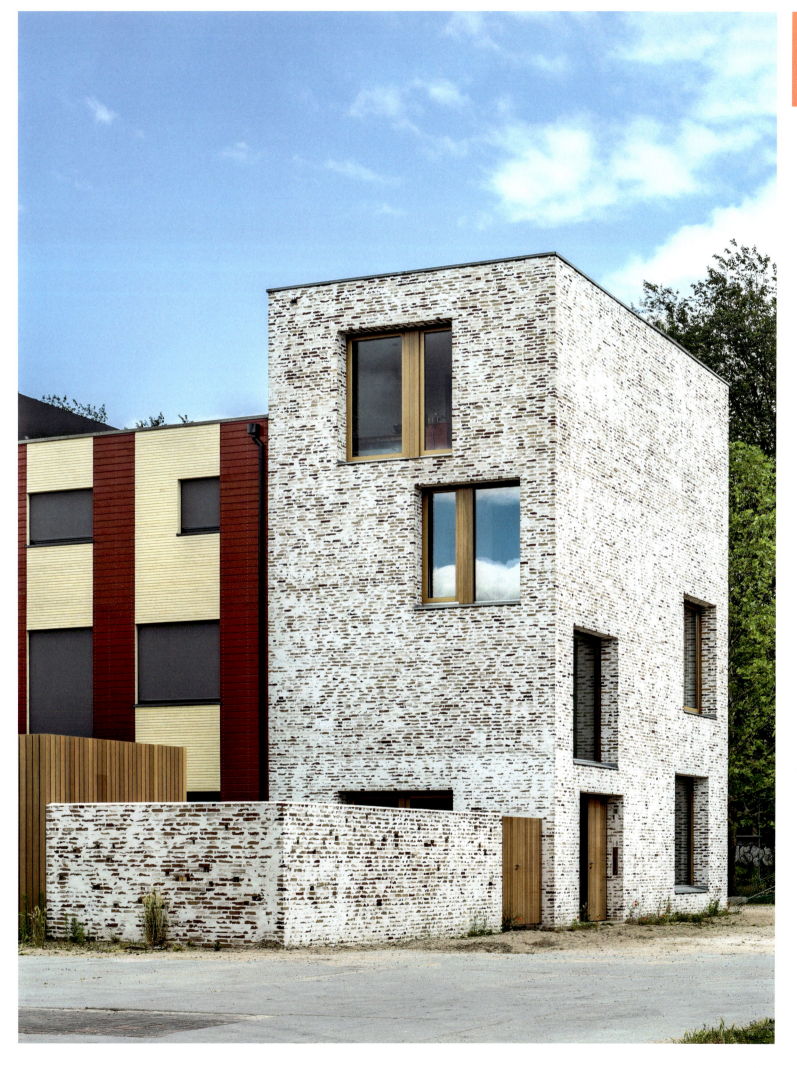

House Koopvaardersplantsoen Amsterdam

The bricks that were used come from different leftover batches.

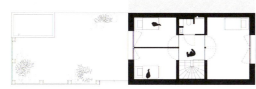
Third floor

Second floor

First floor

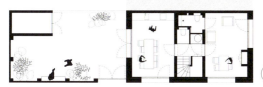
Ground floor

Living together

68	ISABELLA LEBER **Housing Construction in Times of Densification**	96	MANGOR & NAGEL **Falkoner Allé 118**
72	AVENIER CORNEJO ARCHITECTES **88 housing units + 1 retail space — Rue Danton, Pantin**	100	POWERHOUSE COMPANY **Merckt**
80	SERGISON BATES ARCHITECTS **Harbour Building Antwerp**	104	VERS.A **Mexico**
84	HILBERINKBOSCH ARCHITECTEN **TV Tube Factory**	108	WIRTH ARCHITEKTEN **Hulsbergspitze**
88	WINGÅRDHS **Basaren**	112	AILTIREACHT ARCHITECTS + DTA – DEREK TYNAN ARCHITECTS **Grattan Court East**
92	DEHULLU ARCHITECTEN **Social Housing: 34 Single-Family Homes in Zwevegem**	116	A2O ARCHITECTEN **Sky One**
		120	ORANGE ARCHITECTS **Transformation PTT Building**

BRICK 22 Category Winner (applies to entry 72: Avenier Cornejo Architectes — 88 housing units + 1 retail space — Rue Danton, Pantin)

ISABELLA LEBER

Housing Construction in Times of Densification

Isabella Leber

The Clinker Image
The clinker brick in residential construction spans epochs, typologies, scales and continents. As a strictly repetitive element, the clinker forms an ornament without force, and functions in all scales and variants of building, from solid brick to insulating brick, from double-shell constructions with facing shells to the brick slip, which also contributes its share to the "clinker brick image." It overcomes the contrast between diversity and homogeneity, and "is usually able to give the buildings a patina from the outset that distinguishes them from the smooth, aseptic new structure."[1]

The History
A historical model for the goals of current residential construction could be the Gründerzeit era (ca. 1850–1900). At that time, like today, "the need for living space grew in the course of industrialization; entire city districts were newly erected 'in the green field.' Along with apartment houses for the rapidly growing urban population […], quarters with villas and palaces for the rich bourgeoisie also emerged."[2]

Today as well, in addition to multi-story apartment buildings, one cannot completely imagine the latter typology of villas without it, even if it has fallen into disrepute, because it refers to an archetype of residential construction from the palaces of antiquity (from ca. 1900 BC), to Roman complexes, up to Palladio (1508–1580). It had already existed in variance in ancient Greece, one thinks, for instance, of Priene (4th century BC),—a densified settlement concept made up of courtyard houses.

The Problem
The issue of densification is more present nowadays, especially in cities, than it has been for a long time, but is likewise gaining importance in rural areas, where urban sprawl overshadows evolved village structures.

On the one hand, the apartments should become smaller and smaller to generate variably utilized floor space with communal areas and to activate social contacts. On the other hand, the multi-story apartment building should also accommodate the needs and desires of the single-family house, today's counterpart to the villa, and lead to a concept of balance between public and private, living and green space, as well as individual versus community.

Models for this also exist, for example, in England, a country in which the private ownership of living space is deeply anchored. In the 1970s, a time of a great housing shortage in London, experiments were carried out in different parts of the city. Concepts such as the Lillington Gardens in Westminster (1972, Westman, Darbourne & Darke) proved successful: "Known for its staggered elevations, generous courtyard style green spaces and red-brown brick, it is widely regarded as an archetypal high-density, low-rise scheme."[3]

Even today, for economic and ecological reasons, there has to be as much densification as possible to create more and more living space with ever smaller footprints. But how is increasing density also socially and spatially compatible? This is where the clinker brick comes into play, because of its small size, which affords so much space for variance, it often breaks down very large scales to smaller, more humane dimensions.

This is also the case with the Free Trade Wharf complex in London's Docklands (1987, Mathias Alcock), which in its size and solidity would certainly appear far more monumental and less individual without the clinker.

But such megastructures do not correspond to the current zeitgeist, which strives for heterogeneous urban development with many actors, participation and diversity.

However, a problem also lies in today's complexity of requirements and participants: It quickly leads to a cacophony of styles, atmospheres and spatial placement.

Current Trends

This conflict seems to be wonderfully resolved in one of the projects in this book, the Harbour Building in Antwerp, a block divided into five building parts, from the hands of three architectural offices. The connecting element here, as well as a related architectural stance, is the clinker brick. Similar to the Gründerzeit era, it brings together different architectural handwritings into a common language with different dialects. One part of this block is the quayside harbor building, which "takes inspiration from industrial quayside buildings in terms of its massing and presence, and from residential mansion blocks in its detailing of repeated undulating forms."[4]

It thus builds a bridge between scales and typologies. In the interior of the garden courtyard, it is a large, concise volume, facing partly compartmentalized maisonettes, thus forming a heterogeneous ensemble of diverse uses and densities. The differentiation in plinths and the various heights of building volumes, as well as the ornamental use of clinker, also support the connection of the building's five parts.

The solitary Hulsbergspitze building is also a mediator between scales. With its spacious, stepped terraces, the structure quite obviously realizes the idea of one's own home with private outdoor space. Located on a triangular plot of land that closes off the street, it forms an urban hinge "between the Gründerzeit suburb of Bremen, large-scale buildings from the post-war period and dispersed urban structures."[5]

Besides the residential buildings in Antwerp and Bremen already discussed in this book, the "Merckt" in Groningen probably also lies in a price segment that does not address the problem of the housing shortage for low-income earners. Instead, it deals with another current urban development task, namely the revitalization of inner cities. The corner building in the most central location lends the city new impulses through a public ground floor with a food market, a bar on the roof and the private residential wing in between, which anticipates an eclectic revitalization of the center through mixed usage. The materiality of light-colored clinker brick with arcade arches in the base area strives to insert and further write the aesthetics of the historical city center of Groningen.

Likewise, the 88 Housing Units on the Canal de l'Ourcq in the banlieues of Paris are linked to the industrial history of the site via the clinker brick façades, while they are typologically located in a very unique way as stepped solitaires between the urban plaza, canal and romantic communal garden. In addition to the various incisions and protrusions in the balconies, loggias and terraces, the structural, but varied handling of the clinker brick reinforces a granularity that strives for the atmospheric opposite of a large form. As a result, the three buildings, which do not occupy the corners but rather the edges of the triangular construction area, appear without any dominance and yet as a concise urban ensemble.

Despite the high density and urban presence, the dream of owning a home with a private outdoor space and a garden, often damned by architects, is also realized here for low-income earners. In this way, living in these buildings overcomes social and monetary boundaries. How beneficial for society! What a role model for the future!

1 Marlowes; Materialverliebt und detailbesessen, Christian Holl, 13. Juli 2021*
2 Wikipedia; Gründerzeit*
3 Residents' experience of high-density housing in London, K. Scanlon, T. White, F. Blanc, June 2018
4 Sergison Bates Architects, Harbour building Antwerp Belgium, 2021
5 Wirth Architekten, Hulsbergspitze, Wohn- und Geschäftshaus in Bremen, 2021*

* Transl. BD

AVENIER CORNEJO ARCHITECTES
88 housing units + 1 retail space — Rue Danton, Pantin

Christelle Avenier and Miguel Cornejo

ARCHITECT/S
Avenier Cornejo Architectes, Paris/France

LOCATION
Pantin, France

BUILDING PURPOSE
Apartment housing

CONSTRUCTION PERIOD
2019

BRICK TYPE
Facing bricks, paving bricks

BRICK
22 Category Winner

Opened in 1822, the 108-kilometer-long Canal de l'Ourcq originally served to supply Paris with drinking water. It leads into the city from the east and ends in the Bassin de la Villette.

In the suburb of Pantin, just outside the intersection of the canal with the Paris motorway ring, Avenier Cornejo Architectes erected three buildings with a total of 88 apartments on the canal bank. They stand in a semicircle and, together with an existing residential building and an office building, enclose a small square that opens onto the canal.

> "A brick, a frame, an ornamentation, for a common language, three buildings, three colors, three specific identities for one unit."

While two blocks stand in a communal garden east of Rue Danton, the third block, one story higher with commercial space in its base, is on the west side of the street. All three structures have roughly the same cubature, but their design responds to the shape of the lot and the orientation towards the canal: Each of the three- and four-story buildings, shaped according to the irregular parcel boundary, has a two-story, orthogonal volume. The resulting recesses offer space for roof terraces. Apartments facing the street have loggias and balconies facing the garden.

In terms of the materiality, the three buildings also differ. While the solitary structure is made of red brick, the two garden buildings each have light-gray and anthracite-colored brick façades. What they have in common, however, is the brick type, its processing and the façade design. The façades consist of a grid with slightly recessed fields that appear as if they were woven, with horizontally protruding bricks around the window and loggia openings. Hand-made bricks, laid with hollow joints in the stretcher bond, were used. The window fields, on the other hand, are laid in the Flemish bond, with the header bricks set back somewhat to create a relief effect.

The architects see the three brick colors as modern reactions to the pale yellow of the Grands Moulins de Pantin, built in 1884, which stand a little further west on the canal. Each block also has a different color of metal for the window frames and balustrades: The red brick is complemented by gray metal details, the light gray by green ones and the dark gray by brown ones. The bricks were also used as paving stones for the path that winds around the old trees in the garden.

The ensemble succeeds in creating a synthesis of unity and diversity. Although the individual structures are not identical, they are clearly related to one another. Each building has its separate identity and specific shape yet is also part of the whole. The choice of materials contributes quite considerably to this fact. [ab]

88 housing units + 1 retail space — Rue Danton, Pantin

Jury Statement

"The project is situated in the Parisian suburb of Pantin and with clear references to the heritage of industrial brick buildings in this area. Divided into three different entities, the project is scaled down and allows each block to address its own and unique setting in respect to Canal de l'Ourcq, Rue Danton and the square. Each building has been given a color of its own, but they all three share a vivid and thorough use of brick that highlights the textural qualities of this particular building material. The project exhibits straightforward and clear floor plans with spacious terraces and balconies, which, together with an inviting garden space with various greenery and tall trees, makes it a subtle, yet very powerful project."

Site plan

Three houses, three colors: a distinction that creates indentity.

88 housing units + 1 retail space — Rue Danton, Pantin

Various brick bonds create a lively façade image.

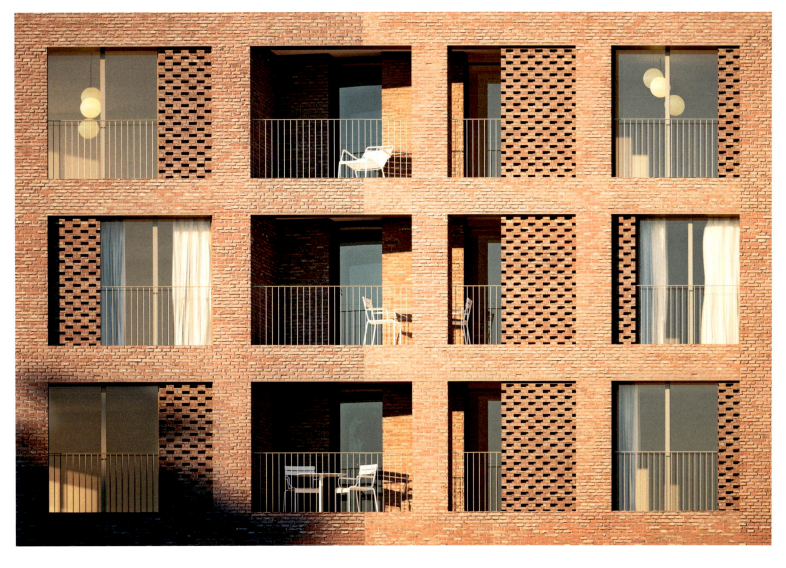

SERGISON BATES ARCHITECTS
Harbour Building Antwerp

Mark Tuff and Stephen Bates

ARCHITECT/S
Sergison Bates architects, London/Great Britain

LOCATION
Antwerp, Belgium

BUILDING PURPOSE
Apartment housing

CONSTRUCTION PERIOD
2018–2021

BRICK TYPE
Clay blocks, facing bricks, paving bricks

Antwerp's Cadix district in is a former port area in transformation. The peninsula to the north of the city center is characterized by a heterogeneous block structure of old warehouses, residential buildings and barracks. For several years now, new, large-scale residential structures have been implanted in this historical fabric — including the Harbour Building, which towers unmistakably next to the quay wall of the Kattendijk Dock. Together with four other buildings designed by Bovenbouw Architectuur and Bulk Architecten, it forms a new city block with a green common inner courtyard. All parts of the structure were designed and materialized differently so that the block offers a distinctive view from every perspective. What they exude in common, however, is an aura of robustness that blends in with the port environment.

Sergison Bates's building contains 70 apartments on four to six floors and, measuring 80 meters in length, takes up the dimensions of the harbor district. At the same time, its angled oriels create a rhythmic structure that breaks up the building's large size and is somewhat reminiscent of the architecture of Victorian "mansion blocks." Only at second glance does one recognize that there are subtle differences in proportions within the repetitive system: The bay windows always protrude pairwise to various extents; while some accommodate a loggia, others belong to the living space behind them.

Ground floor commercial spaces can be found on the dock side under the arcades made of prefabricated concrete elements. Small studio apartments with deep, funnel-shaped bay windows are situated on the courtyard side. Above them, four stair cores provide access to three or four apartments per floor. Residents can enjoy the roof terrace on the lowest part of the building.

> "This is rich, resilient brick architecture, ideal for this great harbour city."

Matching the color scheme of the harbor structures in the area, the architects chose a light-red mottled, irregular brick as the façade material. It is laid in a Flemish bond, with upright rows of bricks under the roof edge and the windows. As a contrast, the back of the building facing the inner courtyard features a gray brick base. However, it does not stop with these two variants, since the closer one gets to the Harbour Building, the more complex its materialization turns out to be. The passage to the inner courtyard is decked all around with diverse textures: two shades of acoustically effective cement tiles on the ceiling, brown clinkers on the floor and a beige brick sawtooth relief on the walls. The elevator entrances, on the other hand, have a base made of blue-green glazed tiles and a brown clinker floor as well.

Mainly used in the transition zones between inside and outside, the hand-crafted materials radiate an almost homely warmth. Thanks to the combination of a solid large shape and loving details, the Harbour Building appears as a friendly giant. [ab]

Harbour Building Antwerp

All parts of the building were designed differently.

In and on the building there is a great variety of different textures.

HILBERINKBOSCH ARCHITECTEN
TV Tube Factory

Geert Bosch and Chris Burghouts

ARCHITECT/S
HILBERINKBOSCH
architecten, Berlicum/
The Netherlands

LOCATION
Eindhoven,
The Netherlands

BUILDING PURPOSE
Apartment housing

CONSTRUCTION PERIOD
2016–2020

BRICK TYPE
Clay blocks,
paving bricks

In 1891, Gerard and Frederik Philips founded a company to produce light bulbs in the Dutch city of Eindhoven. In the next few decades, the once-small town experienced enormous growth thanks to the flourishing Philips Group and eventually became known as the "City of Light." Large factories arose around Eindhoven, including the three industrial areas Strijp S, T and R. The latter was developed in the 1950s as a production site for televisions.

> "With a soft appearance, the brick connects the new district to the industrial past."

In 1997, Philips relocated its headquarters to Amsterdam and started the transformation of the former industrial parks. Only a few industrial structures have survived in Strijp R, including a porter's building, a pumping station and a ceramic workshop, which now houses the studio of designer Piet Hein Eek. Around 500 apartments have been erected, including the RK district with 80 apartments by HILBERINKBOSCH.

The architects like to orient their designs to the history of the place. A television tube factory with sawtooth roofs and 15-meter-long spans was originally located on the building site in Strijp R. The architects used the contours of the factory as a leitmotif for the design of the district. Reflecting the transverse halls of the old factory, the so-called sawtooth houses form its heart. Their concrete dividing walls have a planning grid size of 7.5 meters. A sawtooth roof, which traces the dimensions and shape of the former factory roofs, lies over each of the two residential buildings. Three cross streets cut through the sawtooth pattern and each lead into a collective inner courtyard. The eastern edge of the property is lined with terraced houses, the staircases, kitchens and bathrooms of which are housed in separate tower volumes with long window slits that step somewhat out of line. They allude to the cooling towers of the old glass melting furnace. A four-story apartment block, the design of which is inspired by the architecture of the old Philips office buildings, completes the ensemble.

Made of a light gray, lightly sintered brick with a hand-shaped look, the façades are combined with greenish-beige aluminum panels and window frames. The glazing bar division is based on the old steel window frames of the Philips buildings. Each of the three inner courtyards gains its own identity through the integration of façade panels in one of the light colors of red, green or blue — a further allusion to the television history of the area.

The design develops a language that makes numerous references to the history of the location. Although some elements are quite literally derived from the earlier development, they have a high degree of abstraction, which creates a very modern-looking ensemble. The combination of light gray brick and beige anodized aluminum also skillfully maintains the balance between industrial and homey aesthetics. [ab]

TV Tube Factory

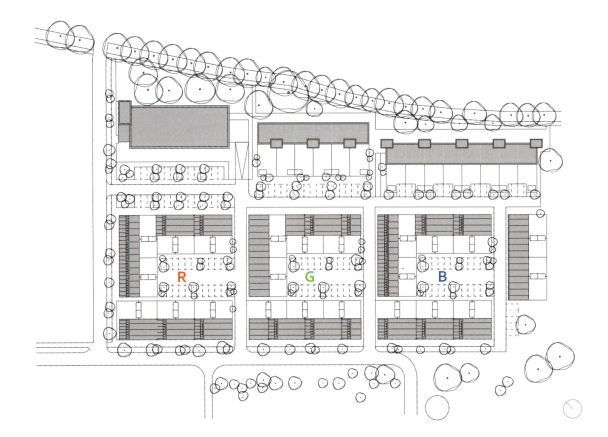

Site plan

Red, green and blue panels serve as references to the TV tube manufacturing that took place here.

The complex unites literal and figurative references of the site's industrial past.

WINGÅRDHS
Basaren

Gert Wingårdh

ARCHITECT/S
Wingårdhs, Stockholm/Sweden

LOCATION
Stockholm, Sweden

BUILDING PURPOSE
Apartment housing

CONSTRUCTION PERIOD
2016–2018

BRICK TYPE
Facing bricks

The first thing one notices about Basaren, an all-white apartment house in Stockholm's historical Kungsholmen neighborhood, are its bold, round volumes. Recalling the aesthetics of Sweden's 1930s functionalism, the house offers an unusual reinterpretation of a traditional urban block on a long, narrow site between two streets on Hantverkagatan hill. To reduce the dominance of the building over its surroundings, the house has been divided in two from the fifth floor onwards: a seven- and a nine-story tower, both ending in semicircular curves. The sober language of functionalism is carried on in the window and door openings on the façades and the continuous railings of the balconies that run parallelly on all floors. The empty wall space and parapet above the top floor openings speak most strongly of references to the inter-war aesthetics in the spirit of Gunnar Asplund or Sigurd Lewerentz.

> "The white, rounded brick house is a response to the airy location."

The apartment building replaced a three-story market structure—an old Basaren—that had stood on the site from 1934 on. The new development was led by the housing cooperative SKB (Stockholms Kooperativa Bostadsförening), a non-profit tenant association that builds and manages property in the Stockholm area and rents out apartments to its members. There is a high interest in this model that offers a more affordable alternative to the mainstream choices of the rental market. Members pay an annual fee to stay in the queue and apartments are rented out to the first ones in line. Basaren has 44 apartments, from 30-square-meter studios to over 100-square-meter-large, three-bedroom ones. The narrow site provides all apartments access to the south-facing balconies while the upper floors of the building offer a view to the sea. As the loop of the balconies wrapping the building is decentered in relation to the main volume, the width and size of the individual balcony space changes gradually, with larger ones in front of the living rooms and narrower ones for bedrooms. Round forms also dominate the interiors of the apartment spaces, where living rooms and master bedrooms have been placed behind the circular ends. A spacious entrance to the building on the ground floor is on the side of Baltzar von Platens gata, with additional common space and bike storage, and more public functions, including a restaurant on the side of Hantverkgatan.

Brick has been used here in the tradition of Scandinavian minimalism—it emphasizes the quality of its details and hidden nuances, using grayish-white, soft-molded stone that has a hand-crafted quality. Upon closer look, each stone is characterized by an interplay of different hues. The plinth of the building is clad with the same white bricks which, however, are glazed here, giving that street front a sleeker character. The ventilation ducts above the main entrance are hidden behind custom-made decorative bricks with oval perforations, repeating in the architects' words the building's elongated elliptical plan. [ak]

Basaren

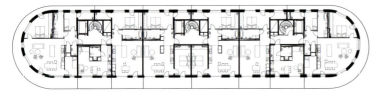

Third floor

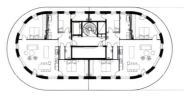

Seventh floor

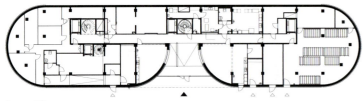

Ground floor

DEHULLU ARCHITECTEN
Social Housing: 34 Single-Family Homes in Zwevegem

Bert Dehullu

ARCHITECT/S
Dehullu Architecten, Ghent/Belgium

LOCATION
Zwevegem, Belgium

BUILDING PURPOSE
Social housing

CONSTRUCTION PERIOD
2018–2020

BRICK TYPE
Facing bricks

Many Flemish towns give travelers and passers-by the cold shoulder in the form of straight, closed street façades, often with lowered shutters. Life takes place at the back of the houses, where private gardens and individual additions and extensions can be found. When designing a social housing estate on the outskirts of Zwevegem, Dehullu Architecten decided to reverse this principle. Projections and recesses in the volumes, as well as carports in front, create an interesting play of shapes on the street side, while the garden side is formulated much more soberly.

Lined along a street and spread over three parcels, the 34 residential units are interrupted by a small cross street and a private plot. The two- or three-story row houses measure six meters between the axes. With the exception of the rows that border the private property, there is a twelve-meter-wide unit at each end of the house rows with two stacked apartments accessible from the garden side.

Each of the row houses has three or five bedrooms respectively. At the entrance, across a width of four meters, the ground floors are set back two meters, creating a sheltered space. The entrance door, however, is not in the main façade, but in the side wall. This enabled the main façade on the ground floor to be completely glazed so that one can see through the houses and into the garden. At the point where the carport roof connects to the house, the upper floor, on the other hand, recedes. In six of the houses a third floor, bundled in three pavilion-like roof structures, is placed above.

> "The authenticity of the brick contributes to the sculptural quality of the project."

All residential units—including the apartment buildings—feature a private, half-walled garden and a shed at the rear. In front of the rows of houses are small gardens and the carports, each standing on a slender leg. Like the floor slabs visible on the façade, they are made of precast concrete components. For the façade, the architects chose a beige, mottled, very lively brick, which they came across by chance: It lay in large piles as leftovers on the factory floor. The producer had made it a long time ago but couldn't sell it and actually wanted to grind it up. The inexpensive bricks were glued in the stretcher bond with joints only eight millimeters wide. They are combined with window frames and doors made of dark, anodized aluminum.

In this way, an elegant, small estate, which at first glance does not reveal how inexpensive it was built and that the apartments are affordable even for the less well-off, was created with simple means. The projections and recesses bring a playful element into the row, while the materialization ensures uniformity, but also vividness at the same time. [ab]

Living together

Site plan

MANGOR & NAGEL
Falkoner Allé 118

Bente Priess Andersen

ARCHITECT/S
Mangor & Nagel, Copenhagenn/Denmark

LOCATION
Copenhagen, Denmark

BUILDING PURPOSE
Social housing

CONSTRUCTION PERIOD
2017–2020

BRICK TYPE
Facing bricks

Brick buildings of various typologies have been characteristic to Copenhagen's architecture since the medieval times. In the city's affluent Frederiksberg district, going back to the 17th century, deep red and copper brown bricks cover the façades of several churches, public palaces and numerous housing blocks. In 2016, the local municipality held a competition for public and permanent refugee housing in a centrally located plot on the corner of Falkoner Allé and Ågade. The tender was won by architects Mangor & Nagel together with the social housing organization Boligforeningen AAB and the engineering company Oluf Jørgensen. The scale and form of the new brick-clad structure is set by its historically significant surroundings. From the eastern side, the house is flanked by the dark-brick national romantic Church of the Deaf; on the northwest, the house completes a row of five-story apartment buildings from the early 20th century; in the courtyard on the south side, the site meets a low structure of a kindergarten. Negotiating carefully between these different sections, the building meets its neighbors on Ågade as a five-story-high apartment house, receding gradually under a long sloping roof to two stories on the courtyard side.

The new house accommodates fourteen apartments, ranging from 69-square-meter-large, two-bedroom flats to spacious, 106-square-meter-large, three-bedroom homes opening towards the busy street. As the architects were operating on a budget considerably smaller than in residential construction for private developers, the detailing of the interior spaces is straightforward, yet architectural solutions have ensured their uniqueness, perhaps even honesty. The low slope of the roof provides pleasant skylights for living rooms underneath and offers unusual room configurations for the inhabitants. In the courtyard wing, the apartments have their entrance from galleries that also function as balconies in front of the living rooms. Due to a lower floor height compared to the early 20th century housing, the new structure makes a small, downward step in the street front towards Ågade. This is compensated by the carefully composed patterns of the brickwork aligning itself with the neighboring building: The base is marked by a rhythm of projecting brick courses, separated from the main body by a soldier course; the window frames in the main part are decorated by a pattern of projecting bricks. In this way, the new façade blends into the existing street, while still maintaining its difference.

This difference is not merely a formal feature. As social and refugee housing situated in an upmarket district with spacious boulevards and fashionable restaurants, the building indicates a shifting approach of the municipality in supporting diversity of class and ethnicity in their neighborhood. Against enclaves of any kinds, either of immigrant communities or of the wealthy citizens, the housing on Falkoner Allé makes a statement about consolidation: of a process that brings different cultures and strata together, while respecting their difference and caring for the existing context. [ak]

"With its warm brick façade, the new building respectfully greets its older neighbors."

Falkoner Allé 118

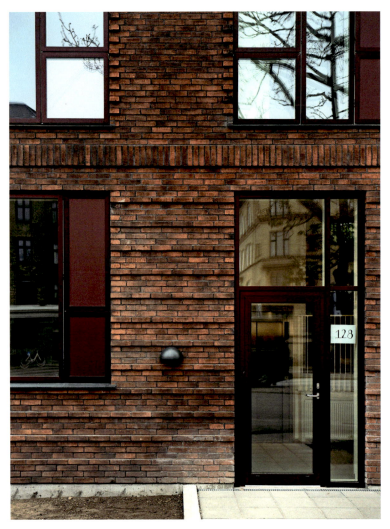

Site plan

98

On the side facing away from the street, the number of stories is reduced from five to two.

POWERHOUSE COMPANY
Merckt

Stefan Prins

ARCHITECT/S
Powerhouse Company, Rotterdam/
The Netherlands

LOCATION
Groningen,
The Netherlands

BUILDING PURPOSE
Apartment housing

CONSTRUCTION PERIOD
2017–2021

BRICK TYPE
Facing bricks

The Grote Markt (The Great Market) is the central square in Groningen. New structures have emerged in recent years on its east side—including the Merckt House, which shows in an expressive way how urban architecture can combine modernity and historical context. Today it is hard to believe that the potential of the area around the Grote Markt between St. Martin's Church and the City Hall had not been used for years. But remedial measures have been taken in the past few years: Forum Groningen, a new cultural building towering like a large rock, was erected next to the church, and the demolition of existing objects gave the square the shape and area it had before the Second World War.

"Echoing history in a locally sourced and parametrically designed façade."

At the end of the new eastern row, the Merckt apartment house now stands between the market square and Forum Groningen. It leads to the adjacent streets as well as to the newly created square in front of the Forum, the Nieuwe Markt (The New Market). Both the design, featuring high, two-story, concrete arches, and the public uses on the lower floors correspond to this urban spatial function: A large supermarket and a restaurant were accommodated here. The cantilevered prefabricated components from which the arches were created have various shapes. With a differentiated cantilever, they adapt to the urban situation and offer a covered area at the sloping corner. The height of the base reacts to the listed building next to it. Moreover, the house is staggered so that it has eight floors facing the square and three floors adjoining the existing structure on Poelestraat.

Eighteen apartments can be found on the floors above this base zone. Here, the façade is made of a light brown, waterstruck brick that picks up the color of the house that once occupied this location. This façade is also sculpturally wrought: The regular lattice structure is accentuated by prism-shaped volumes, and open loggias give the building a varied depth. Golden metal strips are worked into the vertical elements, which lend the house a precious appearance and contrast the horizontal structure of the brick bonds. In cooperation with the concrete element manufacturer, the façade elements were optimized in such a way that the bricks incorporated into them could be kept thin, thus saving material. For the windowsills, on the other hand, tailor-made brick sizes were developed and produced.

The railing and the attic are characterized by a brass-golden metal that complements the color of the brick, allowing it to come even stronger into its own. Articulated in a contemporary architectural language, the building's top floor is nonetheless traditionally divided into a base, middle section and upper end, without having to resort to historicizing means. [ch]

Merckt

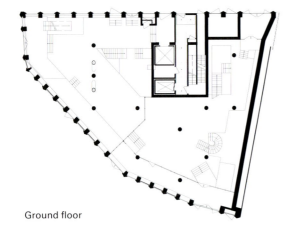

Ground floor

First floor

VERS.A
Mexico

Kobe Van Praet and Guillaume Becker

ARCHITECT/S
VERS.A, Brussels/Belgium

LOCATION
Brussels, Belgium

BUILDING PURPOSE
Social housing

CONSTRUCTION PERIOD
2016–2020

BRICK TYPE
Facing bricks

This innovative social housing project is located in the Brussels municipality of Molenbeek, an area which has a controversial past. After the deindustrialization in the 1980s it deteriorated and became a site for unemployment and riots, but has seen dynamic growth and diversification in its inhabitants over recent years. Thus, any architectural intervention has an impact on the neighborhood in general and spatial decisions carried out during the design and construction phase influence the formation of the future social climate. The architects from the Belgian office VERS.A have recognized their authority and approached their task with extra care for the neighborhood. Contrary to the brief by the local municipality who commissioned the project (the architects were chosen on the recommendation of the chief architect of the Brussels region), they decided not to close the whole street front with the new building, but to move it to one side of the plot and leave the rest of the area for public use, with an already existing large tree in its center. The new building appears to withdraw to one side, giving maximum surface to the new, small, green oasis in the middle of a dense row of houses on the surrounding streets. The quadrangle is separated from the busy street by a wall with three equally-sized, large openings, allowing views to the garden from the street, but also making it possible to close it off for the night and provide security for the inhabitants.

> "The project deals with the tree as an opportunity to open the park and the urban block on the street."

The program of the house consists of three apartments. The ground floor home has one bedroom and a private terrace to the north; it is intended for a user with reduced mobility. From the second to the fourth floors there are two spacious duplex apartments for larger families, with four bedrooms on one level and a living room and kitchen alcove on the other. All bedrooms and the living room open towards the green space in the east; the living room and the kitchen have a spacious corner loggia with views to the street and the adjacent green courtyard.

The architectural language here is minimal, one could say almost austere. Yet, the chosen material of red brick, Flemish bond brickwork and thick, light-gray seams give it a strong presence and contextual influence that relates it to traditional row housing. This is architecture that stages itself consciously as the background to the urban nature and the activities in the green park zone, but through this it claims agency in the city more broadly. On the further end of the brick wall separating the courtyard from the road stands the exotic name of the street in metal letters—Mexico. It is an amusing call to the green zone with typical plants and greenery of the Belgian climate. But perhaps it is also a promise of new kinds of relationships that could emerge there, more sincere and relaxed. At least these are the associations that a northerner might have with the name of a tropical country. [ak]

Mexico

The living area extends over the length of the house and also features a loggia.

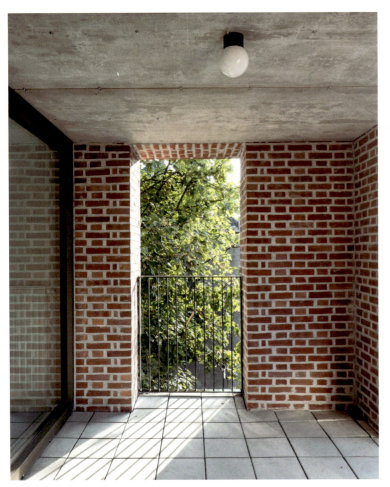

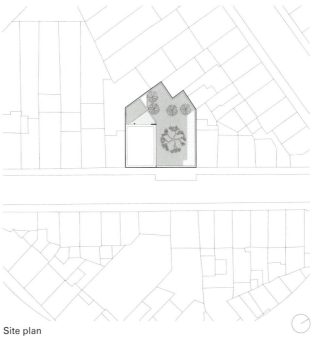

Site plan

"Pocket park": A small oasis in the densely built-up area

WIRTH ARCHITEKTEN
Hulsbergspitze

Jan and Benjamin Wirth

ARCHITECT/S
Wirth Architekten BDA Partnergesellschaft mbB, Bremen / Germany

LOCATION
Bremen, Germany

BUILDING PURPOSE
Apartment housing

CONSTRUCTION PERIOD
2020–2021

BRICK TYPE
Facing bricks

There seems to be a consensus among developers and their clients about what constitutes a good high-end apartment building in 21st century Europe. It would include a façade composed as a minimalist artwork, materials and details connoting transparency and luxury, a rational floor plan with rooms in right angles, large windows and terrace spaces, especially on the upper floors. The Hulsbergspitze apartment building seems to go against this consensus in many aspects. Situated on the meeting point of five streets in historic Bremen, close to the tram stop Am Hulsberg, the location could be seen as a meeting place for the unified urban fabric of the Gründerzeit Östliche Vorstadt (Eastern Quarter) with the more incoherent post-war buildings. This context is interpreted by the Wirth Architekten in a way that is unpretentious and surprising at the same time. Its irregular hexagonal ground floor layout follows the shape of the narrow street corner. On the upper levels the floors protrude and withdraw in shapes and volumes that adapt to the context in an intuitive rather than strictly rational way. Equally, the window and terrace sizes vary floor by floor, and asymmetrically placed eaves articulate the division of the floors on the façade, leaving an impression of almost self-generating forms that have evolved to this shape over a longer time. This seemingly disorderly composition is, however, kept in balance through the consistency of its simple detailing — sand-colored vertical railings and window frames — and the overall sandstone brick cladding of the walls.

The six-story house was built after a winning entry for a local real-estate developer. The program includes fourteen apartments ranging from 30-square-meter-large studios to a 157-square-meter-large penthouse and a commercial space on the ground floor. Intended primarily for the rental market, all apartments come with in-built kitchen units and parquet floors. The apartment configurations continue the complexity of the exteriors, going against the grain of standard rectangular spaces. With different room heights and asymmetrical shapes, the interior offers alcoves and recesses that follow the geometry of the meandering walls.

> "Scale, shape and bricks form an integrated sculpture."

The brick slip cladding was installed for the house only as a second choice after pure plastered walls were discussed. The outcome, however, is a success, speaking to the local typical material and continuing its use in a contemporary form. Contrary then to the ready-made schemas of international real-estate developers, we could speak here of a vernacular approach in a sense of how the term was originally used — speaking a local language against the homogenizing lingua franca of global modernism. [ak]

Hulsbergspitze

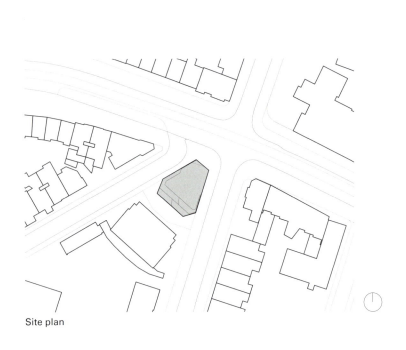

Site plan

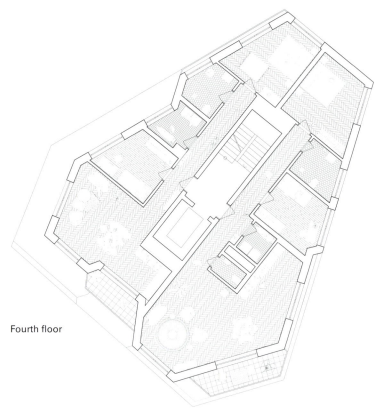

Fourth floor

The building structure and the cream-colored brick façade lend the house an elegant impression.

AILTIREACHT ARCHITECTS + DTA – DEREK TYNAN ARCHITECTS
Grattan Court East

Allister Coyne

ARCHITECT/S
Ailtireacht Architects +
DTA – Derek
Tynan Architects,
Dublin/Ireland

LOCATION
Dublin, Ireland

BUILDING PURPOSE
Multi-family housing

CONSTRUCTION PERIOD
2016–2018

BRICK TYPE
Facing bricks

Grattan Court East is located in Dublin's city center, just a few hundred meters from the National Gallery and Trinity College. Despite its central location, the small, angular street was always a bit forgotten, because its appearance was determined by anonymous garage entrances and the backs of residential and office blocks. At the point where the street bends at right angles, there was originally a single-story parking garage. Now there is a complex with five four-story terraced houses and two maisonette apartments. Historic townhouses in the wider area served the architects as inspiration for the design.

"Brick reinterpretation, reminiscent of the Georgian style."

On the ground floor of each house there is a carport that seamlessly merges into a patio-like garden. Due to the irregular shape of the property, the size of this outdoor space varies from house to house. The glass doors of the carports, which mark the transition between public and private space, but still offer insight are unusual. In addition, on the ground floor there is a bedroom or study with a window facing the street, behind it a bathroom and a staircase. It leads to the first floor with two further bedrooms and from there to the second floor, where there is an open living and dining area with fixed glazed, panoramic windows. Above that there is another study or living room, through which one reaches the roof terrace.

At the eastern end of the row, the street bends and the residential complex also continues at a right angle. There is a further volume with two stacked maisonette apartments that share a carport. The lower apartment has access to the private courtyard on the ground floor, while the upper apartment has a private roof terrace and can be reached by elevator.

The architects used a traditional, reddish-mottled waterstruck brick as the façade material, as can be found in many old commercial areas in Dublin, combined with anodized aluminum window frames.

The result is an ensemble whose cubatures appear very modern, but which, thanks to the brick, also has a handcrafted touch. In its hidden location, it almost looks like a small village — in the middle of Dublin. [ab]

Grattan Court East

The new terraced houses gave the small "back alley" a completely different, yet familiar face.

Garage entrance

A2O ARCHITECTEN
Sky One

Team a2o

ARCHITECT/S
a2o architecten, Brussels and Hasselt/Belgium

LOCATION
Leuven, Belgium

BUILDING PURPOSE
Apartment housing, retail

CONSTRUCTION PERIOD
2017–2020

BRICK TYPE
Facing bricks

What would context mean in a former industrial area that is rapidly turning into a hotspot for stylish residencies and trendsetting stores? Would new architecture align itself with the sobriety of the grain silos and warehouses already in place, the infrastructure that has brought the area its significance in the past, or the glamour of commerce and loft living that characterizes the present transformations? The Sky One apartment and retail building in the Vaartkom area in Leuven has had to position itself in relation to these concerns. It is located at the beginning of the Leuvense Vaart—the Leuven-Dijle Canal that is a historic waterway connecting the Flemish city with the river Dijle and then the Scheldt, flowing to the North Sea. In the past, it was a place for famous beer breweries like Artois, grain mills and timber merchants. At the beginning of the 21st century the district gradually lost its original function and, since 2007, has been the largest urban renewal area in Belgium.

> "The sculptural volume is emphasized by the extensive use of brick."

The new Sky One building on a corner plot between Engels Plein and Vaartkom street seems literally to negotiate the different forces that are at play on the site. The first five floors occupy the whole width of the plot, with commercial spaces on the ground floor and apartments from the second floor onwards. These apartments extend throughout the volume, with living rooms facing the harbor area in the south and bedrooms opening to the more closed northern side. From the sixth floor upwards, the structure changes its shape and becomes narrower, with two apartments per floor as a result of building regulations that determined the percentage of built area per floor in relation to height. The consistency between different parts is visually achieved through the use of a long and narrow, light-gray brick as the main finishing material that was specially developed for the project. Protruding horizontal bands of brick masonry articulate the division of the floors and tie the volumes together into one whole. The projecting indoor terraces and deep-set windows add dynamism to the building, but also provide shade in hot summers. There are no symmetries here; the balconies of the lower block seem to extend and withdraw according to the geometry of the site. Yet, there is a logic that reflects the spatial division of the apartments, six per floor in the lower block, that are of equal width and where the gradual narrowing of the site is reflected in the diminishing sizes of the living rooms. The flats in the house range from 56-square-meter, one-bedroom homes to 118-square-meter ones with two bedrooms and a private swimming pool on the roof.

This is a luxurious apartment house, carried out with utmost care for details and materials, where the surfaces of the tailor-made brick speak of skillfulness and beauty. From its spacious terraces and windows the inhabitants will, over the coming years, witness more transformations of this former industrial area. But perhaps they will also recognize the concealed layers of the building's context, ways of distributing and organizing spaces that have traced the outline for the present changes. [ak]

Sky One

The uniform brick "dress" connects the parts of the house with one another …

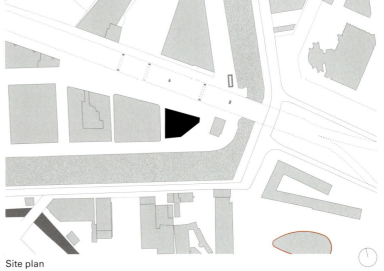

Site plan

... and the horizontal ribbons provide orientation.

ORANGE ARCHITECTS
Transformation PTT Building

Jeroen Schipper, Tess Landsman and Bas Kegge

ARCHITECT/S
Orange Architects,
Rotterdam /
The Netherlands

LOCATION
Rotterdam,
The Netherlands

BUILDING PURPOSE
Apartment housing

CONSTRUCTION PERIOD
2019

BRICK TYPE
Facing bricks

Until the 1990s, the Binnenrotte Square in Rotterdam was not a square, but an elongated leftover space under a railway viaduct. When, after the Second World War, an office building from PTT Telecom, located on a street parallel to Binnenrotte, was to be expanded with an automated machine hall, the decision was made to erect this new structure with its back to the viaduct. In 1951, the brick building based on a design by Jan Koop opened its doors.

At the end of the 1990s, the railway was laid below ground and the viaduct torn down. More and more of the surrounding structures are oriented towards the resulting square, but the automated machine hall still gave it the cold shoulder—until Orange Architects received the commission to transform the hall into residential housing after it had remained vacant for over ten years.

> "… it was our goal to maintain the building's sturdy brick identity…"

The aim was to accommodate 20 studio apartments in the building without sacrificing its industrial character. That is why the architects decided to insulate the walls from the inside and combine it with a thorough cleaning of the dark clinker brick façades. A new entrance hall, an elevator and a wooden staircase were implanted on the inside; all apartments feature an impressive ceiling height of 4.5 meters.

Beyond that, the opening of the monotonous south façade facing the Binnenrotte area posed the greatest challenge in the transformation. All windows received new window frames; some were converted into large French windows with skylights. Terraces for the top floor apartments were cut out of the south side of the roof, which is completely covered with photovoltaic shingles. On the third floor a long balcony, which protrudes somewhat over the head of the building and is clearly recognizable as an addition, hangs in front of the façade. Framed by reused bricks, the former ground floor windows have become the patio doors of a restaurant. All new elements—window frames, railings, balcony, entrance portals—are made of black-brown metal, which reflects the brick building's robust aura.

Telecom machines are still housed in the basement of the building; their waste heat is used to preheat the tap water and the underfloor heating. Electric heat pumps and the photovoltaic shingles and solar boilers on the flat part of the roof cover the remaining energy requirements.

The architects succeeded in making the new interventions visible, without having them define the image. The rationalistic brick architecture has been preserved and only had to forfeit a little of its factual seriousness to open up to the new usage type and Binnenrotte Square. [ab]

Transformation PTT Building

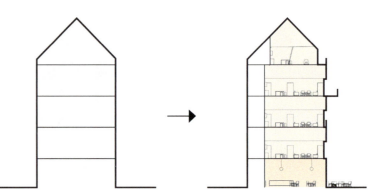

The function changed, but the industrial character has been retained.

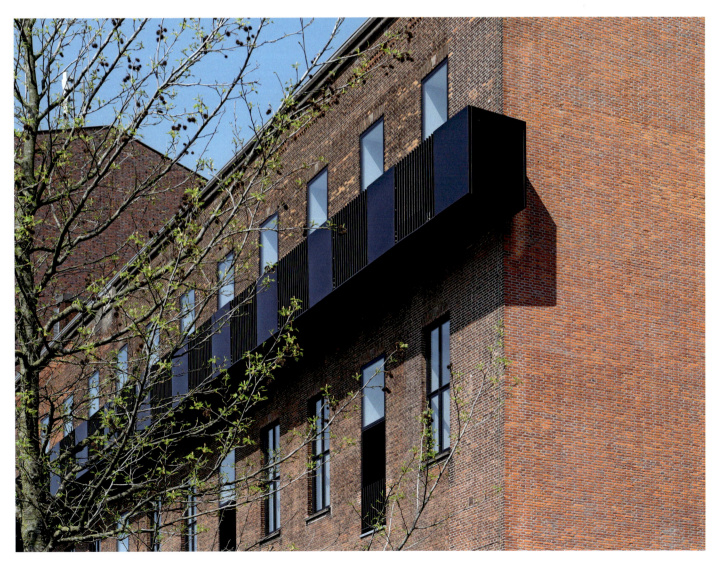

Working together

126 MATEVŽ ČELIK
Office Architecture and Ecology:
Re-assembling Bricks in a New Way

130 BAUMSCHLAGER EBERLE ARCHITEKTEN
2226 Emmenweid

138 VTN ARCHITECTS
Viettel Academy Educational Center

142 JKMM ARCHITECTS
K-Kampus

146 DIEGO ARRAIGADA ARQUITECTOS
Edificio de Estudios

150 TRANSFORM; PLUSKONTORET ARKITEKTER
Vejen Town Hall

154 HOOBA DESIGN GROUP
Kohan Ceram Central Office Building

158 NERI&HU DESIGN AND RESEARCH OFFICE
The Unified City-Schindler City

162 VIRKKUNEN & CO ARCHITECTS
Imatra Electricity Substation

MATEVŽ ČELIK
Office Architecture and Ecology: Re-assembling Bricks in a New Way

Matevž Čelik

In an alarming situation, to seriously tackle the climate and ecological crisis, architecture is facing many challenges. How to deal with excessive energy consumption and pollution caused by buildings? And an even more challenging question: How to reduce pollution resulting from the production of materials in construction? Circular concepts in architecture mean many more buildings renovated for reuse. Circular management in construction means that we will design buildings in such a way that they can be dismantled, and their elements and materials reused. Brick architecture offers all the possibilities for this.

More importantly, bricks also allow many possibilities to assemble them in a way that allows buildings to functionin a significantly different way. In the history of modern office and business architecture, we can observe how maximum comfort has been ensured, how the right atmosphere in the premises was created, for full concentration and efficient work. From the moment corporate owners realized that the success and healthy growth of their companies depend on the well-being and health of their employees, workspaces have been subject to careful planning, up-to-date adaptation to trends in individual industries and the development of the economy. Companies were ready to expend a lot of energy to maintain the comfort, the temperature and clean air in workplaces. But with clever architectural design, the need for this can now even be completely eliminated.

While the 20th century was marked by bright, air-conditioned, boundless floor plans of large corporations, at the beginning of the 21st century, trends in corporate architecture were dictated by global tech companies that grew out of garage start-ups. Proud of their generic workspaces in the form of home rooms and garages, they enforce the aesthetics of rough-hewn and home-style architecture on their campuses; vast air-conditioned oceans of work desks are interrupted by meeting rooms, playgrounds, courtyards, socializing islands, terraces and rooftop parks. The ideal of a glazed, endless floor plan is replaced by less hierarchically arranged workspaces, which keep being artificially heated and cooled.

Today, an even more important change is happening, one that is also visible in architectural designs. With increasing climate and environmental changes affecting our lives every day, we are trying to reduce energy consumption in all possible ways. That is why today air-conditioning engine rooms and ventilation shafts are being replaced by massive walls, shaded, naturally ventilated rooms and other passive elements, which give the buildings a specific new and interesting architectural character. To understand the operation of these constructions, we often look back at history.

The Romans already knew that thick brick walls and floors retain heat energy. Massive brick constructions were used in Roman spas to keep them from getting too cold at night. Today, the massive brick walls are on the rise again, not only to enable pleasant bathing. In Emmenbrücke, Switzerland, the architects Baumschlager Eberle built a five-story building that does not require ventilation, heating and cooling installations. Instead of energy-wasting technology, the architects focused on building physics. They made sure that as much energy as possible was stored in the building in the massive walls. Therefore, they surrounded the building around the perimeter with a thick, load-bearing brick wall that stores heat and stabilizes the internal temperature. The brick is treated on both sides with only a layer of lime plaster. Such a construction allows the office space in the building to be fully heated only by the energy of computers, printers and lamps, and the people who emit their heat into the space. In summer, they do not heat up because the surface of the windows is precisely calculated, and the windows are built into the shady, inner side of the thick wall.

Among Roman inventions, the hypocaust, a central heating system, is even more famous than massive brick walls. The warm air from the hearth in the basement was conducted under the floor and through brick pipes in the walls, thus heating the rooms. But air is also the best insulator, so hollow brick walls perfectly retain heat transfer between outdoor and indoor spaces. In tropical Hanoi, Vietnam, double brick walls protect the Viettel Academy building from overheating from the outside. The architects of VTN designed the academy complex as a series of 12 brick blocks in the middle of greenery, which creates a pleasant microclimate in a tropical environment. The volumes are connected by open corridors and light concrete roofs that provide shade. Largely closed red façades made of rough brick give the complex a strong architectural character. Behind them, a simple construction solution keeps tropical heat out of the building: The double brick walls with a hollow air space ensure that the interior of the building is pleasantly cool, even in hot, tropical everyday conditions.

Among the structural elements of passive brick design, which are increasingly marking the design of office architecture, we also find various forms of blinds. Architects design different types of brick curtains, screens and shutters to shade workspaces. The office building of an Iranian brick manufacturer in Tehran, where it can be extremely hot in summer, is designed as a monolith made of bright orange brick. In this case, sun protection is an essential element of architecture. Hooba Design architects clad the building with specially designed bricks which allowed them to integrate sliding shutters made of perforated brick elements. Thin bricks with round openings can serve as building blocks of blinds, and if the openings are filled with various transparent materials, they filter the light in the rooms in an intriguing way. The space between the blinds and windows is intended for plants that have a positive effect on the indoor climate. When the blinds are closed, due to the depth of the façade wall, they act as a double façade. They retain solar heat while allowing air to circulate and cool on the façade.

In the near future we can expect more and more architectural solutions of this kind. We will also be increasingly encouraged by various green and ecological policies, with which humanity is still too slowly tackling climate and environmental challenges. Many of these policies address energy use and the various challenges associated with it. Architecture can show in a tangible way how theory can be translated and brought to life in the real world. Like in these cases, smart architectural design can make it possible to significantly reduce energy consumption and at the same time create attractive and high-quality spaces.

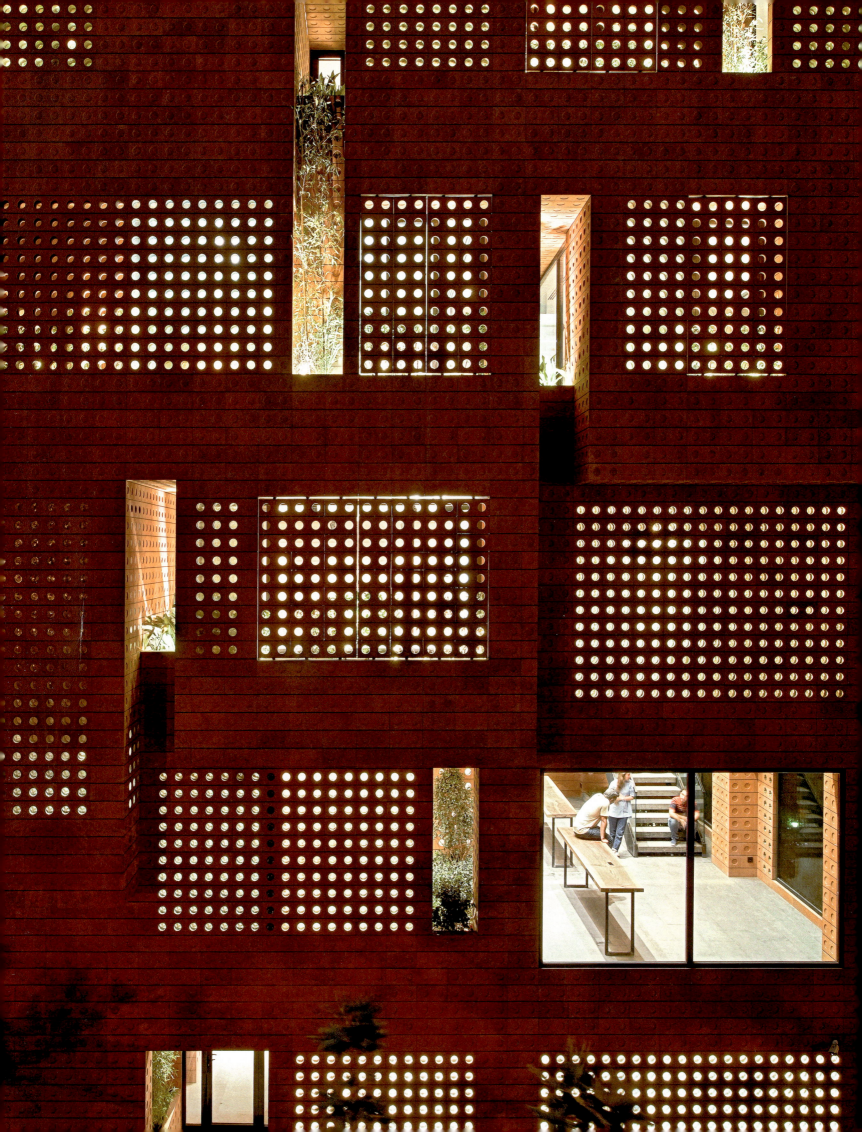

BAUMSCHLAGER EBERLE ARCHITEKTEN
2226 Emmenweid

Stephan Marending

ARCHITECT/S
Baumschlager Eberle Architekten, Zurich/Switzerland

LOCATION
Emmenbrücke, Switzerland

BUILDING PURPOSE
Offices

CONSTRUCTION PERIOD
2017–2018

BRICK TYPE
Clay blocks

BRICK 22 Category Winner

2226 Emmenweid was erected in a historic industrial quarter in place of an industrial building from the early 20th century that would no longer have been worth renovating. The architects call the building technology concept they developed "2226" because it ensures a stable interior temperature between 22 and 26 degrees Celsius. Following a prototype built in 2013, the office and administration complex in Emmenbrücke, Switzerland, further integrates this construction principle, which cools and heats solely through structural effects.

> "The idea is to achieve as much comfort using as little technology as possible."

Closely coordinated with monument preservation, the new structure takes on important attributes of the previous one in terms of area, roof design and cubature. While the appearance of the old building was characterized by red brick, the new one stands out with its light-colored lime plaster and the regular arrangement of the spacious windows set deep in the walls. The building's solidity is emphasized by its four stories and a hipped roof without a roof overhang—and that is not an aesthetic end in itself, since the mass of the walls is the idea on which the house is based. An incision in the volume creates a distinctive contour line that structures the massiveness, alludes to its predecessor, and establishes a reference to the neighboring buildings.

The floor plan is conceivably simple and devised to allow a wide variety of uses. Around an inner zone with stairs, sanitary facilities and tea kitchens, there is a wide, flexible area without load-bearing partition walls, which can be flexibly designed as required. The wall structure consists of two layers of bricks, each 36.5 centimeters thick, one as loadbearing and insulating, the other solely as insulating. Large, unfilled blocks of bricks, which ensure efficient vapor diffusion and whose high storage mass contributes significantly to keeping the climate inside stable, were used. In addition to the walls, the exposed concrete ceilings factor into the storage mass. As the simple construction foregoes additional technology and relies entirely on architectural means, it promises to be particularly durable. This also takes into account the heat emanating from lighting, computers and people. Furthermore, the deep reveals that shade the interior are part of the concept. The precast concrete windowsills feature two-centimeter-deep troughs in which the rainwater can collect and evaporate. Rainwater damage is to be avoided in this way. Only the ventilation is sensor-controlled to regulate the fresh air content and humidity. The interior design underscores the principle: high quality, unobtrusive, open to what is coming. [ch]

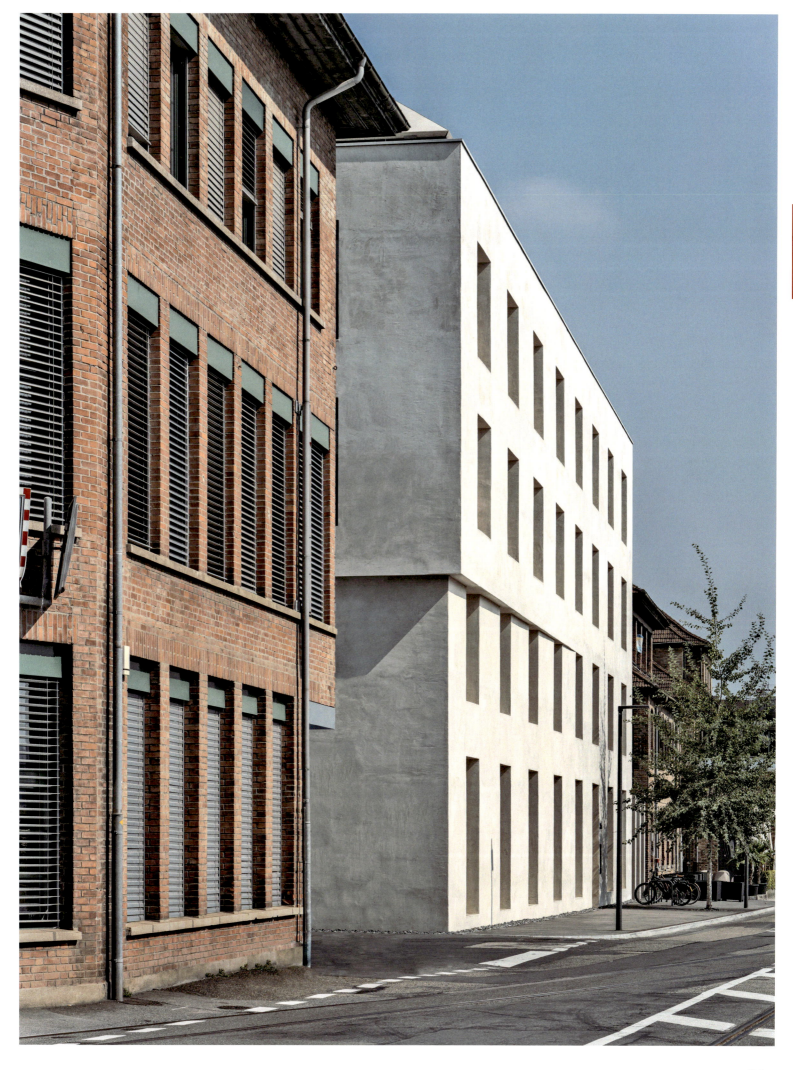

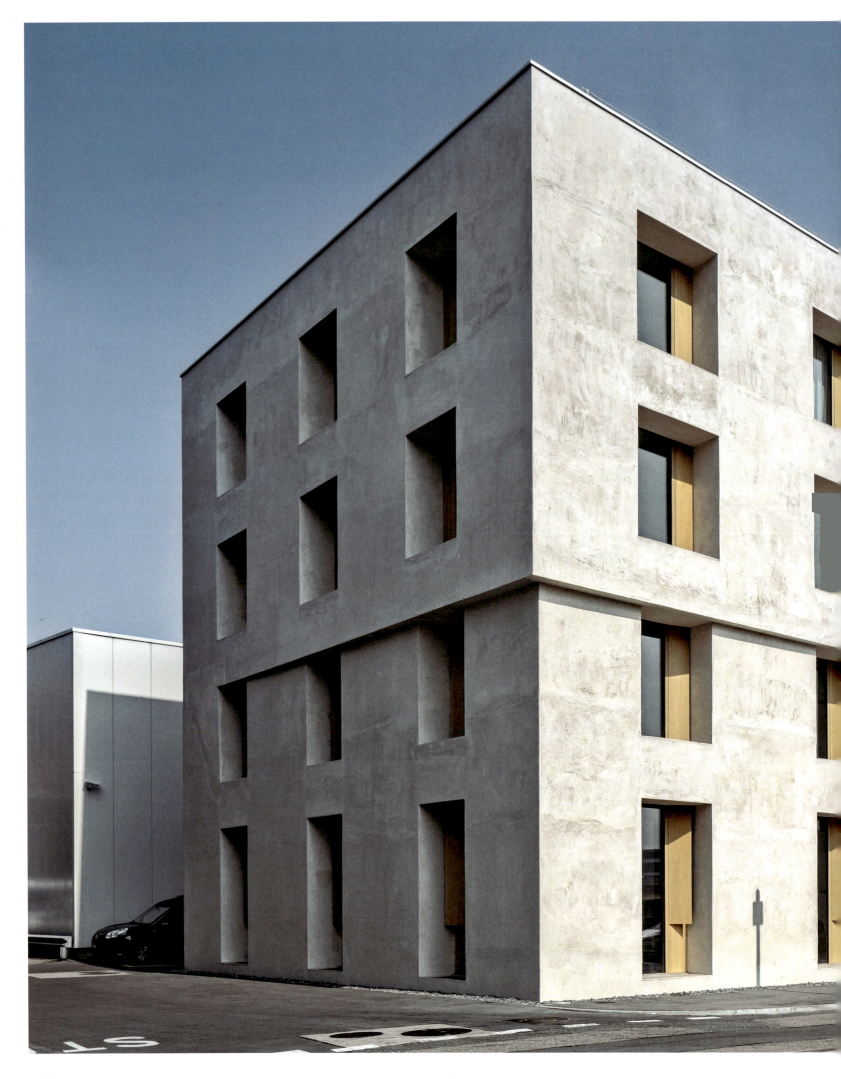

2226 Emmenweid

Jury Statement

"With Baumschlager Eberle's 2226 Emmenweid project, completed in 2018, a design that focuses on the performative properties of brick masonry and thus makes an important contribution to the question of architecturally high-quality sustainability is honored. Brick masonry is able to develop spatial qualities without being visible. In European architectural history, brick plays an outstanding role as a construction material for urban buildings, even where it does not come into view as exposed masonry. With the 2226 Emmenweid project, which builds upon the experience with the 2226 Lustenau project by Baumschlager Eberle, this historical construction form is updated in a contemporary way: A double-skinned brick wall consists of a load-bearing and an insulating shell, each 36.5 centimeters thick, with a brick specially optimized for the respective purpose and open to vapor diffusion. Here the structural and physical attributes of the brick are fully utilized to obtain, with solid plastered masonry, a year-round, climatically stable architecture, lending it a sculptural appearance in the urban realm. The deep reveals characterize the building from the outside and create effective sun protection. At the same time, the inertia of the storage mass enables a stable climate between 22 and 26 degrees Celsius to be maintained in the interior throughout the year: without heating and without cooling. The simple-looking structure impresses with its cubature and proportions, as well as its spacious floor plans, which are open for use thanks to the load-bearing outer wall in conjunction with a load-bearing core. Dispensing with short-lived components in the façade, extension and housing technology ensures that this building will be long-lasting, need little maintenance and therefore meet optimal energy efficiency requirements. Besides the spatial and atmospheric qualities, 2226 Emmenweid shows that a new way of thinking is possible in commercial office construction; a way of thinking that, in overcoming the mechanical age, brings the factor of time into focus: a long service life and year-round and all-day climate stability."

Around the massive core there is a wide, flexible usage zone without pillars or load-bearing partitions.

2226 Emmenweid

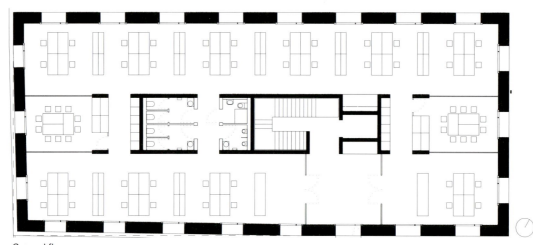

Ground floor

The external appearance was closely coordinated with the monument protection authority.

Deep window reveals provide shade.

VTN ARCHITECTS
Viettel Academy Educational Center

Vo Trong Nghia

ARCHITECT/S
VTN Architects
Ho Chi Minh City / Vietnam

LOCATION
Ha Noi, Vietnam

BUILDING PURPOSE
Education

CONSTRUCTION PERIOD
2016–2018

BRICK TYPE
Facing bricks

Located in the Hoa Lac Hi-Tech Park 30 kilometers west of Hanoi, the Viettel Academy serves as a training center for the largest Vietnamese mobile network operator. Deliberately built on a secluded site outside the city, the building complex forms the heart of a campus facility featuring accommodation and training spaces. Employees take part in advanced training courses and longer training programs here.

The Viettel Academy consists of twelve cubic building volumes of different sizes, in which classrooms, meeting rooms, lecture halls and offices, but also a library and a cinema are housed. The auditorium is in the largest block, the security service in the smallest. The taller structures have four to five floors, the lower ones two to three floors. Almost all of them stand in the water, since a shallow basin extends between the blocks, which in warm, humid Vietnam benefits not only the aesthetics, but also the microclimate. Corridors, ramps and stairs connect the individual buildings at various heights. The most spectacular feature is the skywalk on the concrete structure, which stands on slender steel supports on the third-floor level between the cubes and provides shade in the outdoor area. In some places it touches the buildings, in others it maintains a little distance. Not only do a few trees protrude to varying degrees from this concrete platform, but also the individual cubes. Gardens, in several of which even trees are growing, green the roofs.

"With an innovative design concept, Viettel Academy is one of the largest modern constructions built with raw bricks in Vietnam."

Differently sized window openings that appear to be randomly distributed break up the façades of the individual structures, which are double-layered and made of local red brick. Thanks to their unusual bond, they have a strong texture: Every second brick is turned 90 degrees and projects a little out of the wall. The brick walls and structural elements made of concrete are also visible inside. There, however, the walls have no texture, but are laid in a simple stretcher bond.

The design thrives on contrasts: red brick and green gardens, structured brick walls and reflective water surfaces, massive cubes and an elegant flying roof. Through the integration of trees, gardens and water areas, the campus exudes a lot of calm, while the play with various layers and volumes brings life into the ensemble. What basically arose was a small village whose individual houses are connected on different levels by paths. [ab]

Viettel Academy Educational Center

The aereal photo shows the clear structure of the complex, which is so diverse inside.

JKMM ARCHITECTS
K-Kampus

Juha Mäki-Jyllilä

ARCHITECT/S
JKMM Architects, Helsinki / Finland

LOCATION
Helsinki, Finland

BUILDING PURPOSE
Offices

CONSTRUCTION PERIOD
2016–2019

BRICK TYPE
Facing bricks

The keywords most often associated with Scandinavian Modernism include minimalist aesthetics, accommodation of light, and democratic provision of space. K-Kampus, a new office block for the Finnish retail conglomerate Kesko by JKMM architects, seems to embody all of these principles and bring them together with the social and technological demands of the 21st century. Their new building for 1,800 employees is located in Eastern Helsinki, in a former fishing harbor area that has recently seen rapid growth and conversion into a modern living and working neighborhood. The seven-story structure is on a reinforced concrete and steel frame and features white brick infills that alternate with large, undivided window spaces. The sequential rhythm of the slanting brick surfaces, laid in situ, give the house its specific character. Their oblique geometry reappears on the narrower ends of the block, where on the southern side an asymmetrical recess forms a small square in front of the main entrance.

The core of the building is its atrium space, rising through all floors and flooded with light from the glass ceiling above. Upon entrance to the atrium, the user arrives to a public café, an auditorium space and a multifunctional seating area organized with wooden steps that can function as temporary work and meeting spaces. Here one can draw parallels with magnificent atria in Helsinki by Alvar Aalto from the mid-20th century that aimed to bring the social and physical ideals of Southern urban culture to the context of Nordic climate — National Pensions Institute, the Rautatalo office building or the Academic Bookstore. The K-Kampus office floors that can be accessed further on from the balconies surrounding the atrium are divided into zones according to the needs of the employees. Instead of designated workplaces, there are areas for collaboration, over one hundred negotiation spaces, 1,250 work stations, meeting and presentation rooms. The spaces are finished with oak floors and lined in pinewood; each floor has its own color schema and theme that can be easily identified. A feature that speaks of the needs of the 21th century is the building's energy efficiency monitored by artificial intelligence that keeps the energy consumption at low levels. It is also Finland's first office buildings to be carbon neutral in waste management.

> "The architecture of K-Kampus embodies the core values such as functionality and consciousness, the modernist Scandinavian principles."

K-Kampus relates well to the Scandinavian spirit: it is architecturally daring, carefully carried out and replete with references to Finnish architectural history. But through this it also imagines other spaces: piazzas oriented towards ample sunlight and filled with casual conversations of the inhabitants, spaces for commercial exchange and democratic access. [ak]

K-Kampus

The recess in the building creates a forecourt situation and marks the entrance.

All functions are arranged around a central atrium.

DIEGO ARRAIGADA ARQUITECTOS
Edificio de Estudios

Diego Arraigada

ARCHITECT/S
Diego Arraigada Arquitectos, Rosario/Argentina

LOCATION
Rosario, Argentina

BUILDING PURPOSE
Offices

CONSTRUCTION PERIOD
2018–2021

BRICK TYPE
Clay blocks, facing bricks, paving bricks

The city of Rosario in Argentina has a rich architectural culture going back to the times when it was the country's main grain port in the late 19th and early 20th century. At the core of this tradition are prominent neoclassical and Art Nouveau public buildings with elaborate decorations and straightforward rhetorical and tectonic qualities. In recent years, a new culture that relies on minimalist aesthetics emphasizing authentic materials and local traditions has emerged from this rich locality. The studio and apartment house by Diego Arraigada Arquitectos grows out from this context and contributes to it in a new, inspiring way.

> "Bricks are split in half, exposing towards the exterior their inner nature."

Located in a dense residential neighborhood, not far from the Parque de la Independencia, the house first had to meet the local building regulations requiring load-bearing brick partition walls between structures. The façades of the house are clad in red bricks that have been manually split in half, with the rough inner side turned outward, resulting in a tactile surface that, in the architects' own words, is both "strange and familiar." The building's façade is laconic from the architectonic viewpoint, articulated solely by the irregular composition of the large, square-shaped windows. For a viewer on the street, this uneven organization of the windows plays a trick—at first, it is difficult to tell the number of floors on the building. In reality, the four-story house consists of two parallel longitudinal bays of studios, with each bay shifted half a level in relationship to the other. Due to the resulting difference in heights, the ground floor and top floor studios vary in their measurements from the regular rooms. Each studio space has two windows, one opening to the front and the other to the side view, a minimal kitchen and a bathroom unit. The spaces with ceilings and floors finished in polished gray concrete, white walls and plywood doors speak of the minimalist aesthetics familiar from art galleries, design schools and avant-garde architecture offices. These are workrooms or short-term residencies for the young, creative urbanites, people not drawing rigid borders between working life and leisure.

On the fifth floor, the common stairwell leads to the roof garden. Inserted between red brick floor and high brick walls in orange, brown and red tones is a rectangular flowerbed with a mixture of plants: some replicating the wild greenery that used to grow on the same site before the house was built, others more cultured, with bright yellow and red blooms. Here is a space for contemplation—cut off from the noises and hustle of the street below and opening to the sky, a reminder of the need to take into account nature's viewpoint in our everyday life, to give it stronger agency, also in the context of architecture. [ak]

Edificio de Estudios

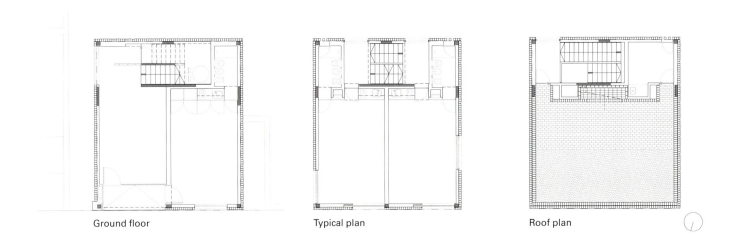

Ground floor Typical plan Roof plan

The façade bricks were cut in half and placed with the rough side facing out.

TRANSFORM; PLUSKONTORET ARKITEKTER
Vejen Town Hall

Lars Bendrup

ARCHITECT/S
TRANSFORM
Pluskontoret Arkitekter,
Aarhus/Denmark

LOCATION
Vejen, Denmark

BUILDING PURPOSE
Offices

CONSTRUCTION PERIOD
2016–2019

BRICK TYPE
Facing bricks

Vejen Town Hall is a laconic yet complex building. Its four-story rectangular volume is carried by a regular concrete structure and the office spaces on both sides of the building are marked by a rhythmic sequence of vertical windows. On the other hand, this uniformity is broken by the large double-height glass door of the main entrance and the asymmetrically stacked windows above it, giving light to the building's atrium and main staircase. On the top floor, a series of larger openings indicate the space where the city council meets. The complexity is further underlined by the ingenious use of light-gray brick cladding, and its asymmetrical perspectival niches around the windows, laid in a sawtooth method. The vanishing point of this imaginary perspectival grid thus formed is the main entrance, oriented towards the town hall square in the east.

As a major public addition to the community of 10,000 inhabitants, the building has a diverse functional program. It provides 184 workplaces for the employees of the municipal offices dealing with urban development, technology, entrepreneurial and environmental issues, among other things. At the same time the town hall has to provide open access and services for the city's inhabitants. Therefore, the ground floor atrium extends throughout the building, connecting the offices around it and the spacious lobby area with a wooden staircase running through all four levels. On the ground floor level the public atrium can be entered from both sides of the building, providing a quick access from the main square or from the parking place on the west. The town hall was erected after a winning entry for a competition with pre-selected participants. It replaced a municipal office building from the mid-20th century, representing with its uniform fenestration and concrete post-and-beam structure the anonymous face of the welfare-state bureaucracy. The new town hall follows the site of the previous building, but adds a stronger symbolic dimension for the place and turns the square in front into a new focal point of the city.

> "We have carefully adapted all façade geometry to brick dimensions for quarter-, half-, three-quarter and whole bricks. No special stones have been used."

Modernist Danish town halls have featured prominently in 20th century architectural history. Aarhus City Hall by Arne Jacobsen and Peter Møller is a regular structure clad outside in gray marble and including a luminous atrium indoors. Søllerød City Hall by Jacobsen and Flemming Lassen is an asymmetrical gray block where the meeting hall is marked on the façade by a set of larger vertical windows. Vejen Town Hall keeps up a dialogue with this monumental tradition through its cladding, atrium space and rhythm of windows. Other influences like the sawtooth bricklaying used in Copenhagen's Louisiana Museum are added, but the changing ideals and needs of small communities in the 21st century are also taken into account. [ak]

151

Vejen Town Hall

A further example of the richness of possible brick ornaments

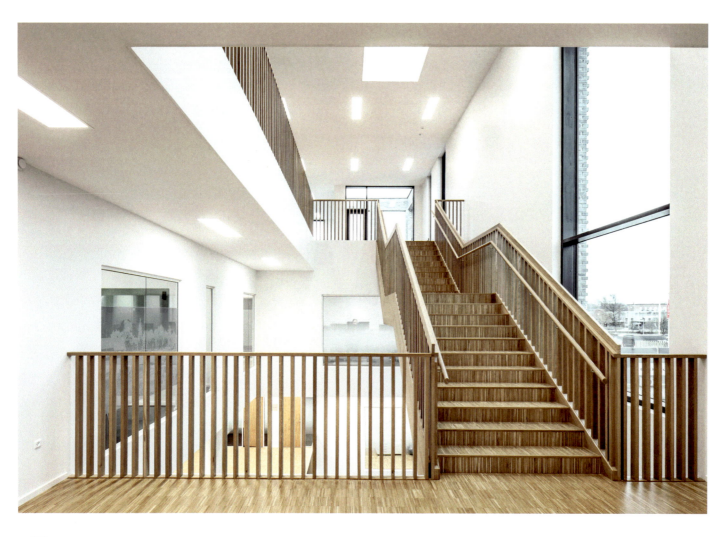

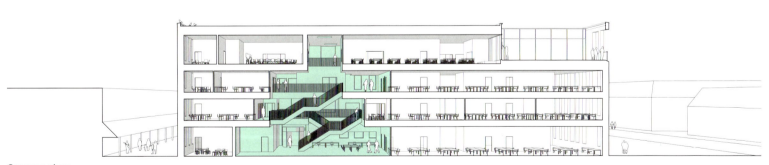

Cutaway view

HOOBA DESIGN GROUP
Kohan Ceram Central Office Building

Hooman Balazadeh

ARCHITECT/S
HOOBA Design Group, Tehran/Iran

LOCATION
Tehran, Iran

BUILDING PURPOSE
Offices, showroom

CONSTRUCTION PERIOD
2016–2019

BRICK TYPE
Facing bricks

The Kohan Ceram building serves as the headquarters and flagship of the Iranian brick manufacturer of the same name. It stands on the edge of a residential area in Tehran, right next to the highway. This location, in combination with the density of development in Tehran, which makes large window openings a rarity, prompted the architects to work with the client to create a special, semi-transparent brick for the structure.

> "The brick module not only forms the façade, but also forms the entirety of the project both on the interior and the exterior."

Although not appearing as such, it is a renovation project. The existing office building was dismantled down to the reinforced concrete skeleton and transformed into a multifunctional new structure. A parking garage is located on the ground floor, the brick manufacturer's showroom on the two floors above, and an office with meeting rooms on the third floor. Occupying the building's two top floors is an apartment.

A red, thin-sized brick with two round recesses was developed for the project. These recesses can optionally remain open, but they can also be filled with two round glass inserts. A pantile version is also part of the series. Using these bricks, double-skinned walls that envelope the entire building were laid in a vertical bond. Especially the side facing the highway is very flat and abstract. Its structure consists of a staggered overhang above the first, second and third stories, as well as vertical slits from which green plants grow. Areas of open, glazed and pantile bricks alternate. The folding shutters in front of the façade openings are also made of double perforated bricks and integrated into the abstract design. When all the shelters are closed, only the three windows of the showroom on the first floor offer a view of the building. The interior walls also feature this brick, so that it also dominates the appearance of the inside of the building.

On the highway side, a second façade with large window openings is hidden behind the overhangs. The sixty-centimeter-deep space is furnished with planters, which fold around corners in some places and penetrate the interior of the building. In some cases, loggias lie behind the folding shutters. A terrace is located on the flat roof. Thanks to the perforated façades, the building is transformed into a large luminous object on the highway in the evening.

The consistently red-colored, double-holed brick makes the building a bit reminiscent of a Lego structure. While it looks very solid from the outside, it turns out to be astonishingly awash with light inside. Not only a successful advertising campaign for the brick manufacturer, the edifice could also represent a solution to privacy problems in densely populated cities like Tehran. [ab]

Kohan Ceram Central Office Building

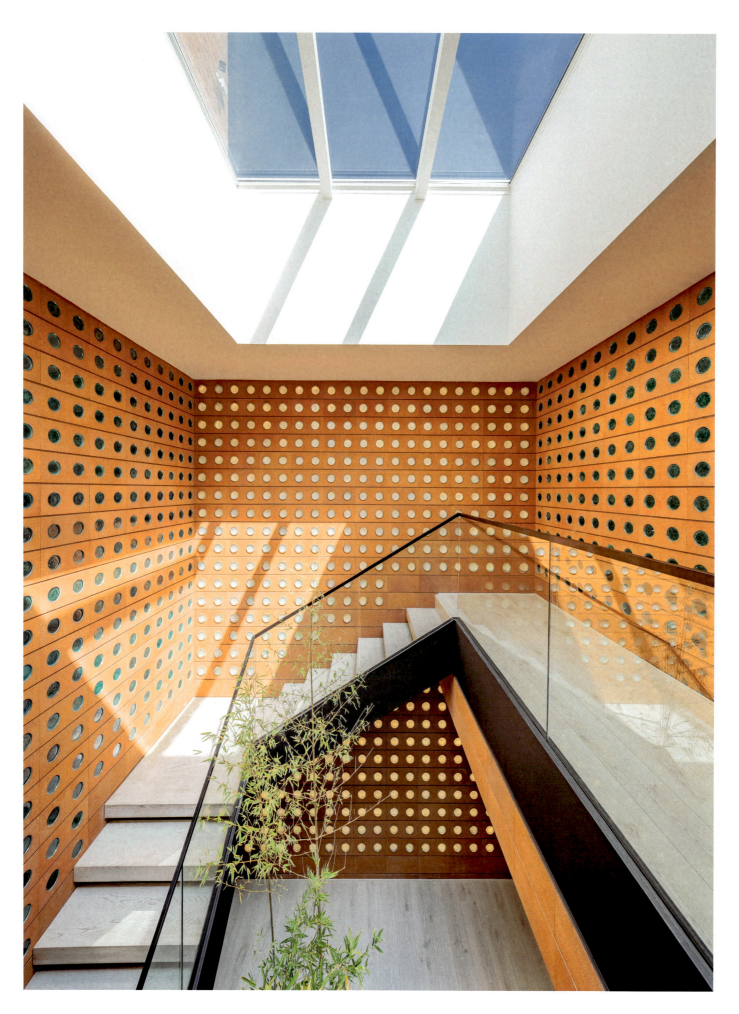

The basic elements consist of specially developed, thin-sized bricks, each with two open, closed or glazed holes.

157

NERI&HU DESIGN AND RESEARCH OFFICE
The Unified City-Schindler City

Lyndon Neri and Rossana Hu

ARCHITECT/S
Neri&Hu Design and Research Office, Shanghai/China

LOCATION
Shanghai, China

BUILDING PURPOSE
Offices

CONSTRUCTION PERIOD
2020

BRICK TYPE
Clay blocks, facing bricks, traditional Chinese bricks

The well-known architecture firm Neri&Hu designed the Chinese headquarters for a large elevator manufacturer in an industrial area in the greater Shanghai area. Situated between two factories, the complex is the new heart of the entire facility: with a research center, exhibition spaces, a training center and offices for 800 employees, including meeting rooms and a canteen with 600 seats. To set a perceptible focus for this spatial program in proximity to the large factories, Neri&Hu developed a figure from a stone base that connects all parts of the headquarters. Contrasting in terms of material and façade structure, three four-story cuboids were placed on its elongated, two-story components to provide office areas. The research and development area that closes the complex in the northeastern end, on the other hand, grows from the base to a mighty rock. A slender tower over one hundred meters high is enclosed by the office and research area and is used for testing elevators.

The office buildings are characterized by black and white façades made of steel and glass. Translucent profile glass panels in front of the actual glass façade are a balancing element of the horizontal structure. This minimalist and elegant façade is a subtle reference to the company's Swiss origins. Each of these three structures features an inner atrium that connects the floors visually and physically.

> "Two million recycled bricks are a physical continuation of material heritage and an archive of the transformation that China is going through right now."

Solid and bricked, the base is completely different. Here, too, atria have been cut in, but laid out as open courtyards that correspond to the open spaces on the roof. The base accommodates the auditorium, canteen, cafés and lobbies. This is not the first time that Neri&Hu have resorted to the gray brick that is widely used in China. The way they deal with this ubiquitous material has become a trademark of the office: On the one hand, because they reuse the material of demolished buildings and thus interweave the past and the present. In this case, over two million bricks from old buildings have been recycled. On the other hand, the architects have developed an inimitable virtuosity in the use of these bricks. The play with large volumes, deep incisions, protrusions and recesses, openings that give an idea of the solidity of the walls, is complemented by one of the surfaces that stretch over the building like a second, independent layer: Variously textured bricks, sometimes dense, sometimes loosely offset against each other, create a wide range of structures that lend the buildings a sense of liveliness and variety. Without negating the solidity of the base and the research and development area, the threatening monotony is countered by a fascinating abstraction. [ch]

The Unified City-Schindler City

The tower ist used for testing the elevators.

The gray brick base evokes the material heritage of the region.

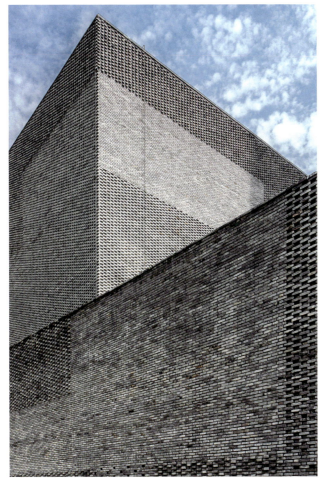

VIRKKUNEN & CO ARCHITECTS
Imatra Electricity Substation

Tuomas Kivinen

ARCHITECT/S
Virkkunen & Co Architects Ltd.
Tuomas Kivinen, Helsinki/Finland

LOCATION
Imatra, Finland

BUILDING PURPOSE
Infrastructure

CONSTRUCTION PERIOD
2019–2020

BRICK TYPE
Facing bricks, hand-made long bricks

One of Finland's most famous natural attractions, the Imatrankoski Rapids were used to generate electricity in the 1920s. The area around the waterfall is one of the landscapes under state protection, but the historic power plant is also listed. Characterized by a restrained classicism typical of the Nordic countries, the hydropower plant building is made of red brick, while the dam is clad with gray natural stone. To enable the natural spectacle of the rapids to be experienced today, the locks of the power plant dam are opened at certain times.

> "Our goal was to further elevate the beauty of the historical site."

Imatra supplies electricity mainly to southern Finland. To be able to operate the power plant according to current standards, renovations and modernizations were inevitable. Built in 1929, the substation had to be replaced by a new structure, which had to be sensitively integrated into the context of the facility, not least because it is accessible from the city. Since the old substation had to be maintained until the new one could be put into operation, the new building was erected on a raised property on the western edge of the site. Together with the existing plant, it encloses a spacious courtyard there. One of the three stories was laid underground to allow the new building to blend into the ensemble despite its elevated position and to not tower above the existing one or the treetops. Inside the reinforced concrete structure is the gas-insulated switchgear. The outer skin consists of a jagged shell of handmade gray bricks featuring slight irregularities in shape, texture and color. The building material references the power station, its color the cladding of the dam. The flat format and the various gray shades of the bricks lend the masonry the appearance of natural stone.

The brick wall is connected to the reinforced concrete wall of the inner shell with a steel frame; the distance between the two shells is large enough to provide space for a maintenance walkway. The brick shell is closed on the lower floor—on the one hand, for safety reasons; on the other hand, it forms a visual base under the upper part of the façade, which is designed as a latticework. Staggered at right angles across the corner, an open and a closed layer alternate on each side of the folded structure here. The latticework structure ensures a varied appearance of the simple building geometry, on the one hand, and natural light in the hall, on the other.

The concrete shell closes at the top with a continuous ribbon of windows. The special size of the brick (528 × 108 × 37 mm) determines the axial dimensions of the zigzag profile, and since the brick is particularly long, the building structure can also be easily recognized from a distance. The bricks had to be cut for the closed wall. To avoid wasting material, brick rubble served as plastering. [ch]

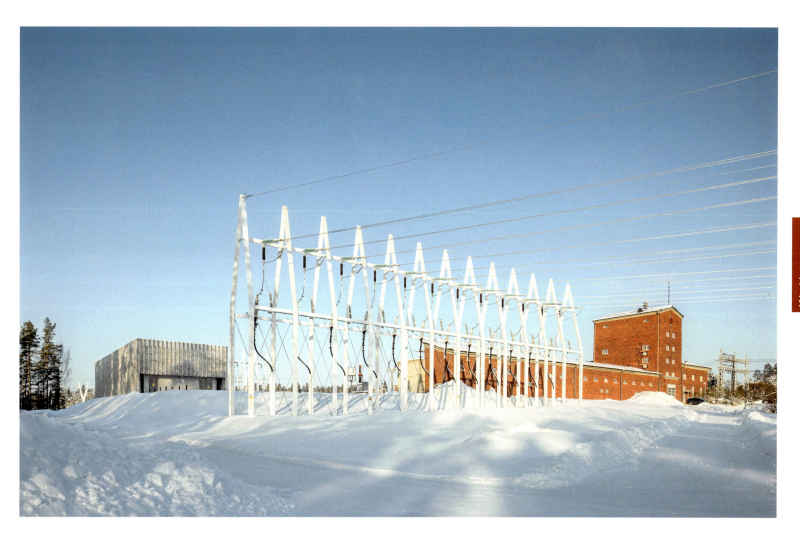

Imatra Electricity Substation

Due to the brick lattice, sufficient daylight enters the interior of the structure.

Sharing public spaces

168 HENRIETTA PALMER
In Search of a Renewed Public Space

172 STUDIO ZHU PEI, ARCHITECTURAL DESIGN & RESEARCH INSTITUTE OF TSINGHUA UNIVERSITY
Jingdezhen Imperial Kiln Museum

180 BAROZZI VEIGA
Musée cantonal des Beaux-Arts Lausanne

184 AIA + BB ARQUITECTES + GGG
Camp del Ferro Sports Hall

188 TRANS ARCHITECTUUR STEDENBOUW, V+ BUREAU VERS PLUS DE BIEN-ÊTRE
Leietheater Deinze

192 A+R ARCHITEKTEN
Project Burma Hospital in Myanmar

196 ANTONIO VIRGA ARCHITECTE
Cinema Le Grand Palais

200 COLECTIVO C733
Matamoros Public Market

204 BRENAC & GONZALEZ & ASSOCIÉS
Rosa Parks School

208 MAGÉN ARQUITECTOS
Auditorium-Theatre in the Old Quarter of Illueca

212 B-ARCHITECTEN & BEVK PEROVIĆ ARHITEKTI
Erasmus University College

216 ZERO ENERGY DESIGN LAB ARCHITECTS
Girls' Hostel Block, St. Andrews Institute of Technology and Management

220 UMARCHITEKT, ULRICH MANZ WITH M. KUNTZ AND CH. GATZ
Jewish Museum Franconia

224 DOMINIQUE COULON & ASSOCIÉS
Housing for the Elderly in Huningue

HENRIETTA PALMER
In Search of a Renewed Public Space

Henrietta Palmer

When the COVID-19 pandemic forced public life to retreat, new light was shed on the city as a public environment. As workplaces, theaters, libraries, bars and restaurants, universities and primary schools were closed, everyday life was pushed back to the home and human encounters were expected to be limited to a close circle. For societies with an already established digital infrastructure, office work, education, entertainment and socializing partly moved into the home screens. In many ways, this was a step in line with the already established 'smart city agenda' — a strategy for digitally managing and monitoring urban choices, movements and interactions via apps and algorithms. With urban public spaces now restricted by curfews and emptied of the ubiquitous mass of tourists, in what appeared to be a joint agreement, the private home was transformed into a new urban cockpit.

As a result of this move, nature (re)emerged as a new destination for public life, at least so in a Swedish context. Due to the so-called right of public access, Swedish nature is by law public and accessible, but despite this existing right the increased presence of people in forests and nature reserves in the immediate vicinity of urban areas was overwhelming. A parking lot next to a public path, which normally does not hold more than a few cars on a Saturday morning, was filled to bursting point; barbecue areas had to be booked in advance; and forest trails were as populated as city streets. In addition to the fact that the access to fresh air and a feeling of escape from the sphere of the home attracted the urban crowds to the forest, we can speculate on what these nature experiences entailed spatially and socially. If we use public space as a kind of prism for our reading, what qualities could be extracted from these experiences to support a revised role of public space in a transformation towards a sustainable society?

In a contemporary discourse on feminist materialism, there is an increased attention to the soil, the growing materials and the artifacts we are surrounded by. These thinkers claim that we cannot separate our lives, thoughts and actions from the material, but these are interconnected and interdependent.[1] The experiences from nature visits during COVID times have increased this awareness. In contrast to the digitalized everyday life, the close encounters with soil, bark, rotting leaves and pine needles provide us with a *new material sensitivity.* This sensitivity, translated into the urban environment, would include an acceptance of both robustness and fragility. However, materials in public environments are more often chosen to withstand human interaction than to invite commitment. But as public space needs to mitigate the consequences of climate change, such as extreme heat or floods, a new sensitivity to material capacity and transformation is emerging. A renewal of public space would therefore mean an increased material awareness that welcomes both permanence and decay.

Reminiscent of this experience is that of sharing time and space with other beings. In many ways, this is the public space modus operandi, that is, providing a spatial condition for different personal, cultural, political and commercial agendas to coexist. But from now on this point of departure is given a holistic dimension where the feeling of being part of a larger ensemble of living beings appears as a new public quality. Although our cities might not contain the nature reserve's myriads of life with its various cycles of life and death, *the feeling of sharing a larger landscape and a longer time horizon* can emerge through the design of public space. Such a perspective brings people together beyond individual rhythms, or, for that matter, beyond commercial trends and seasons, and positions us and our time in relation to both history and the future.

Thirdly, a close reading of the public qualities of the nature experiences leads to something that is often forgotten when we create our cities, which is a capacity *to combine the monumental with the intimate.* In natural landscapes, there is a constant shift of long views and majestic formations, but which also includes protected spaces where human activities take place easily and in a relaxed manner. The experience of something bigger than ourselves rarely falls into our everyday lives, even less now that the home environment becomes our most visited place. At the same time, the need for intimacy is often overlooked in the public space, which has also been reinforced by COVID-19's distance rules. But when you combine the monumental with the intimate, an awe and respect for what we do not understand is associated with what we can understand. Raising this quality to urban spaces would help us position ourselves in relation to what appear to be the incomprehensible challenges of, for example, climate change.

Based on this experience, we can also consider the *public space as a sanctuary.* When the home becomes a violent environment or too crowded for personal development to take place, the public space must be the place where individuals can experience freedom. Just as the natural landscape offers both overview and protection, the public space must accommodate similar qualities. This is also the principle for public institutions such as schools, churches, hospitals and universities where the protection and development of the individual is at the center. To make cities more inclusive, which is even more important in times of uncertainty, public space should offer similar conditions as a non-negotiable alternative to an increasingly digitalized and consumable urbanity.

In some of the nominated proposals in the category of Sharing public spaces we can find qualities that speak to those described above. The public market in Matamoros manages to bring together monumentality and intimacy, both as a public building and as a public place. With distinct architectural features shaped by oversized brick lanterns, and with a small-scale interior that provides space for a mix of activities, the market becomes an everyday haven in a fragmented urban landscape. The Jingdezhen Imperial Kiln Museum is another extraordinary example where monumentality is interwoven with intimacy. The ambiguous exterior shapes along with arched interiors bring to mind excavations of an ancient settlement. The tactility of the brick structures in combination with the ever-changing reflections from the surrounding water mirrors raises a wonder of being part of a mystery that has not yet been explained.

The Rosa Parks school complex in Villeurbanne and the hospital in Magyizin both manage to fulfill the qualities of public space as a sanctuary. Effortlessly located in the urban environment, the Rosa Parks school presents an interior of sheltered balconies for outdoor activities overlooking the schoolyard's secluded tranquility. The hospital on the crest of a hill becomes a reference point in a landscape frequently affected by natural disasters. At the same time, it is a physical and mental refuge for individuals in need of healthcare and their waiting families. The peaceful interior with walls of rough brick and unpainted wood provides an intimacy in a physically stressed environment, comforting worried visitors.

By learning from the experiences from the pandemic, public space can regain forgotten qualities. These are qualities that must not be compromised when societies deal with contemporary and future complexities. The transition to a sustainable society will not be without conflicts and efforts. Therefore, imaginaries that are challenging the ruling paradigm of competition and economic growth must be central in urban transformations, and public spaces created to include, comfort and celebrate life in all its forms.

1 See, for example, writings by Donna Haraway and María Puig de la Bellacasa.

STUDIO ZHU PEI AND ARCHITECTURAL DESIGN & RESEARCH INSTITUTE OF TSINGHUA UNIVERSITY
Jingdezhen Imperial Kiln Museum

Zhu Pei

ARCHITECT/S
Studio Zhu Pei;
Architectural Design &
Research Institute
of Tsinghua University,
Beijing/China

LOCATION
Jingdezhen/Jiangxi
Province, China

BUILDING PURPOSE
Museum

CONSTRUCTION PERIOD
2016–2020

BRICK TYPE
Facing bricks

BRICK
22 Grand Prize Winner

Located in Inland China on the Chang River, the city of Jingdezhen has been an important porcelain manufacturing center for over 1,700 years. The Imperial Kiln Museum was built right next to the Imperial Kiln ruins from the Ming Dynasty and is dedicated to the porcelain history of the city.

> "The local tradition of reusing old kiln bricks mixed with new ones is inherited by the museum."

Eight parabolic brick vaults form the museum building, which has two ground-level and five underground exhibition halls. The cigar shape of the vaults, which all have a slightly different height, length and curvature, is derived from the traditional shape of the kilns. Half of the vaults have glazed ends, the other half open ones. Slightly twisted against each other, the barrel vaults are all arranged side by side on the property in a north-south direction. This connects them to the street grid of the city, but also ensures natural ventilation of the museum in the hot summer months when the cool north wind blows through the open vaults. Five sunken courtyards inside the building also provide a cooling chimney effect.

The entrance to the museum leads between two shallow water basins into a large, vaulted foyer. On the left is a smaller volume with an auditorium, on the right are two featuring a café and tearoom. Offices and supplies are also housed in their own "cigar." Behind the foyer are three exhibition halls with stairs leading to the basement. Further exhibition halls, but also the courtyards, each with its own design theme (gold, wood, water, fire and earth — materials that are needed in the manufacture of porcelain) are also situated there.

The courtyards also serve to direct daylight into the basement. On the upper floor, light falls through the open ends of the vaults, as well as through horizontal slits of light above the floor and slits at the points of contact between the volumes. There are also cylindrical skylights that resemble the smoke holes in kilns. One of the vaults was cut open in the middle to integrate several kiln ruins that were first discovered during construction. Depots and technical rooms are accommodated in a second basement.

The construction of the museum also makes reference to the kiln tradition: The vaults consist of double-shell brick walls built in the traditional way without scaffolding and then poured out with concrete. The 2.8 million bricks used are a mix of new and old ones left over from the demolished kilns, because to ensure that the porcelain kilns retain their thermal properties, they are torn down and rebuilt every two to three years. The resulting demolition bricks have always been reused in Jingdezhen and can be found in the façades of many residential houses and other structures — and now in the Imperial Kiln Museum as well. This means that not only the design and function, but even the construction of the museum pay homage to the porcelain history of the city of Jingdezhen. [ab]

Sharing public spaces

Jingdezhen Imperial Kiln Museum

Jury Statement

"The Imperial Kiln Museum brings to the forefront the reinterpretation of the traditional kilns which are local tradition and local history in China. As the architects work with re-used kiln bricks, they simultaneously honor the production and the material. The structure of the vaults is very specific. It is a repetition of eight volumes that differ in scale and size and are intrinsically connected together in both directions vertically and horizontally. They perform like the last formwork of the whole structure which evokes a unique atmosphere in terms of light and wind. A very complex program ranges from an auditorium to exhibition spaces, a library and a café. The project incorporates everything that makes up the public space, and also redefines the approach to the ming-dinasty's tradition."

Open and closed vaults

Sharing public spaces

Jingdezhen Imperial Kiln Museum

Foyer

Vault, brick and light

Sharing public spaces

Jingdezhen Imperial Kiln Museum

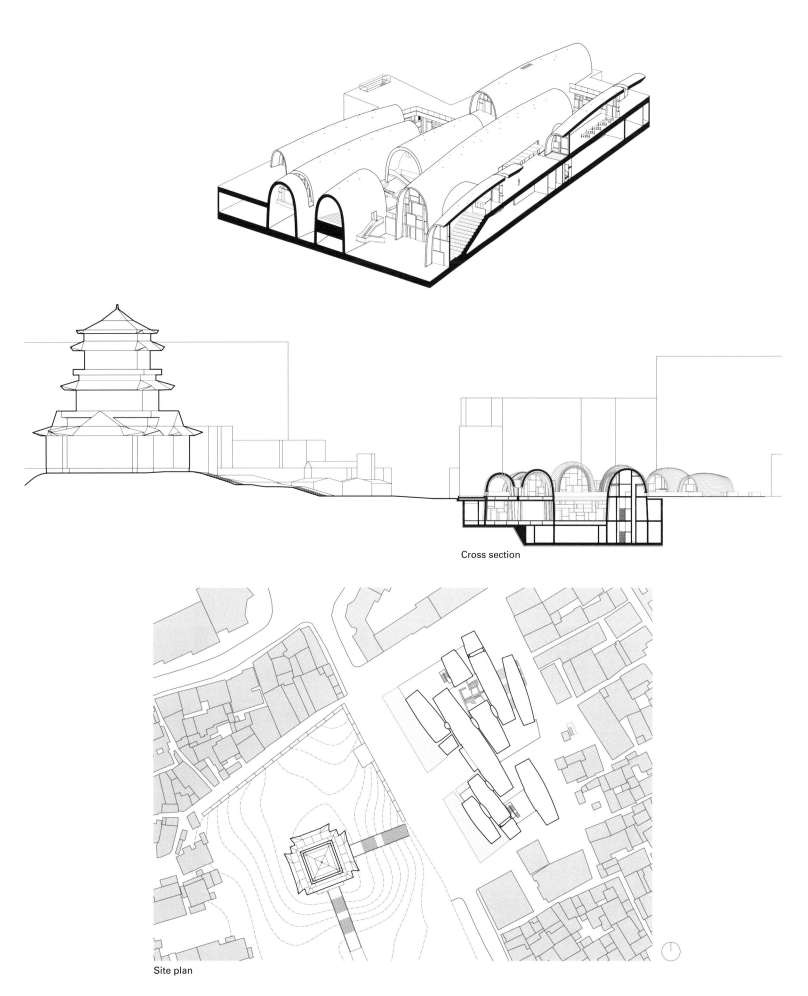

Cross section

Site plan

Auditorium

BAROZZI VEIGA
Musée cantonal des Beaux-Arts Lausanne

Fabrizio Barozzi and Alberto Veiga

ARCHITECT/S
Barozzi Veiga GmbH, Barcelona/Spain

LOCATION
Lausanne, Switzerland

BUILDING PURPOSE
Museum

CONSTRUCTION PERIOD
2016–2019

BRICK TYPE
Facing bricks

The Musée cantonal des Beaux-Arts (MCBA) in Lausanne is part of a new art district emerging not far from the main train station in the center of the city in western Switzerland. With a collection that includes more than 10,000 works from ancient Egyptian to contemporary art, the MCBA is the largest museum in the ensemble, which in the future will also include a museum for photography and one for design and handicrafts. It stands on the southern edge of the site parallel to the railroad tracks and presents itself as a 145-meter-long, monolithic volume made of light gray brick.

Barozzi Veiga, who also developed the master plan for the art district, wants the hard, clear lines of the abstract building to be understood as a reminiscence of the area's industrial past. The references to the history of the location do not end there. Instead of completely demolishing a railway station hall from the 19th century, as initially planned, the architects decided to preserve fragments of the structure and integrate them into the museum building as spolia. One end of the hall protrudes from the closed south façade and, with its arched window, forms an effective contrast to the straight lines of the new building. Another, more subtle allusion can be found on the narrow east façade, where the outlines of an old train station building can be seen — as if the spirit of the place had left its mark on the wall.

> "The Musée cantonal des Beaux-Arts Lausanne is a brick monolith defining a new, continuous public space where architecture becomes the frame of the urban life and the containers of the new public art center of the city."

While the south side of the museum, oriented towards the railway, is hermetically sealed, its north side opens towards the city. Like the train station, it defines the public space and at the same time protects it from the noise of the passing trains. At first glance, the symmetrical north façade with its 22-meter-high, 1.5-meter-deep slats also appears quite stringent. However, specifically positioned window openings are situated between the slats. The façade on the ground floor, where the social functions of the museum with the foyer, bookstore, restaurant and auditorium are found, is the most porous. Inside, the fragment of the station hall proves to be identity-giving, since the arched window determines the shape of the ceiling.

The void in the foyer extends over all three floors. Around it are the exhibition halls, structured by five cores that also have a constructive function. The top floor features a sawtooth roof that lets indirect light into the building and makes a further reference to the area's industrial history.

Conventionally laid in a stretcher bond, the brick that enwraps the entire building was specially developed for this project; its white-gray color matches the light natural stone buildings of Lausanne. Only the slats are made of prefabricated components, which are clad with 24-centimeter-thick ceramic clinker brick slips.

The museum building is a solitary structure with a context. It skillfully balances between the object-like character and the location, between monumentality and haptics, whereby the velvety, light-gray brick plays an important role. With its abstract, rhythmic design, the building is a welcome haven of tranquility in the former industrial area. [ab]

Musée cantonal des Beaux-Arts Lausanne

Integrated historical outlines and fragments

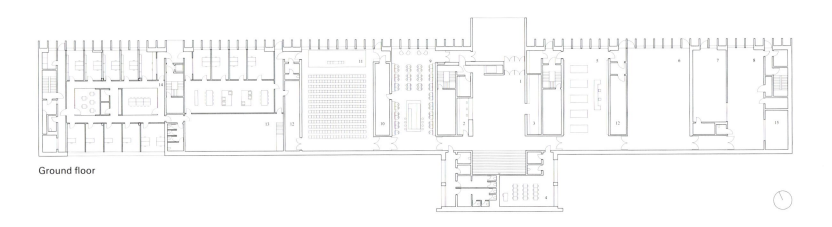

Ground floor

Sharing public spaces

AIA + BB ARQUITECTES + GGG
Camp del Ferro Sports Hall

Gustau Gili Galfetti, Toni Barceló, Bárbara Balanzó, Joan Carles Navarro and Albert Salazar

ARCHITECT/S
AIA Activitats arquitectòniques; Barceló Balanzó Arquitectes; Gustau Gili Galfetti, Barcelona/Spain

LOCATION
Barcelona, Spain

BUILDING PURPOSE
Leisure

CONSTRUCTION PERIOD
2017–2020

BRICK TYPE
Clay blocks, facing bricks, paving bricks, lattice bricks

La Sagrera is a neighborhood in the Sant Andreu district in northern Barcelona, comprised of partly abandoned, partly converted warehouses, factories, and workshops, mixed with apartment blocks. Three new sports courts were to be built on behalf of the city in this transformational district on a relatively small plot of land between two old factory buildings, which now serve as an art and dance school.

Due to the limited space, the architects—a project consortium of three offices—placed two of the three halls below ground. A large public forecourt could thus be created on the roof of the more northerly structure, which lies about two meters above street level. At the same time, the exposed surface of the building was reduced, thereby cutting energy consumption.

With its red brick façade, the structure adapts to its surroundings. To put its size into perspective, open and closed, as well as opaque and transparent masonry alternate. Bricks in various formats and red tones were additionally used. This results in an irregular pattern of bands and stripes, which at first glance appear to be randomly distributed, but in reality are arranged according to the functions behind them. Alternated and sometimes combined with polycarbonate panels, slag bricks act as sun and privacy protection for the sports halls. Angled brick partitions, which provide even more shielding from the sun, are also on the south side. The curvy line of the roof has an almost logo-like character. Its inverted vaulted caps echo the sawtooth roof of the neighboring old machine hall.

Inside, the sports complex can accommodate up to 800 spectators. Since hardly any facing materials were used, its steel truss structure, spanning 35 meters, is visible in the halls. With the exception of the wood-clad foyer, the interior walls are also made of red brick. All smaller spatial elements—café, cloakrooms, storage rooms, installation rooms, balconies—are accommodated in an exposed concrete component located between the two halls.

> "The façades alternate empty and full, opaque, translucent and transparent parts."

A building that makes clever use of the small size of the property and, with its somewhat rough, yet friendly aesthetic, integrates into the structure of the neighborhood, thus arose. The architects want it to be seen as a contribution to the dialogue between the industrial past and the sustainable future of La Sagrera. At the same time, the building has numerous references to the surrounding residential buildings, which are also made of terracotta-colored bricks, and some have brise-soleils made of slag bricks. The sports complex offers the biggest surprise in the evening, when the lights go on inside and the entrance side of the closed shell is transformed into a large lantern thanks to the window slits and the translucent, multi-skin panels. [ab]

Sharing public spaces

Camp del Ferro Sports Hall

Cutaway view

The sports hall is an important urban element in terms of typological and physical presence.

TRANS ARCHITECTUUR STEDENBOUW/V+ BUREAU VERS PLUS DE BIEN-ÊTRE
Leietheater Deinze

Klaas Verdu and Carolien Pasmans Thierry Decuypere and Jörn Aram Bihain

ARCHITECT/S
TRANS architectuur stedenbouw; V+ Bureau Vers plus de bien-être, Ghent/Belgium

LOCATION
Deinze, Belgium

BUILDING PURPOSE
Culture

CONSTRUCTION PERIOD
2015–2019

BRICK TYPE
Facing bricks

The Leietheater in Deinze, a small city in East Flanders, was built after a collaborative winning entry by the TRANS and V+ offices in the international architecture competition organized by the local municipality. In their proposal, the architects suggested moving the structure to a different site from the one in the brief to free up the park space for the citizens and frame the new theater with already existing public buildings— on the one side the museum of fine arts and folklore "Mudel" from the 1980s, and the recently erected municipal services building on the other. Providing space for various performative practices, the new theater is a rectangular structure with the rising volume of the fly tower on the side of the Tweebruggenlaan and the gradually receding volumes of the hall and foyer on the side of the main entrance in the park.

> "The theater has a silhouette wrapped in a brick dress, made up of two types of brick."

Although from a distance this geometry seems rather straightforward, on a closer inspection the building then starts to open up, revealing the abstract detailing with the complexity of ideas behind it.

One already notices the unexpected material pairings in the exterior. The base on the entrance level is composed of glass walls and shiny aluminum panels, above it sits a white brick façade with glazed and matt stones laid in a stretcher bond, with obliquely extruding bricks on every second course. The volumes of the foyer and the hall are finished with the same bricks, now in a Flemish bond with changing minimalist patterns and gradually diminishing amounts of extruding stones. This sequence of the continuities and changes of bricks produces a play of light and shadows on the façade, depending on weather conditions, the time of day and the position of the viewer. Indoors, the foyer space is organized around a large, round light source in the ceiling. Its softly curving edges are covered by a coarse-grained, white plastering, the walls and an elevated walkway below are of gray in-situ concrete. Light effects are more dramatic here, the contrasts between illuminated and dark spaces more defined.

As the architects have indicated, their building is a homage to the Luminist painters in Deinze, especially to Emile Claus, who coined this term as an analogue to French Impressionism and whose masterworks hang in the nearby Mudel museum. Depicting scenes of village life and local nature, the Luminists' main concern was how to capture fleeting effects of light. In some of Claus's paintings light is almost atmospheric: flooding the landscapes and figures on the canvas or defining the geometries of the village houses in a way that air itself becomes perceptible. By analogy, the carefully composed theater building, its juxtapositions of materials, their different surfaces and shades, although representing a different historical moment, make light of the central subject of architecture and intensify the way how the surrounding environment is perceived by its users. [ak]

Leietheater Deinze

Different laying methods create fine gradations and a variety of light and shadow effects on the façade.

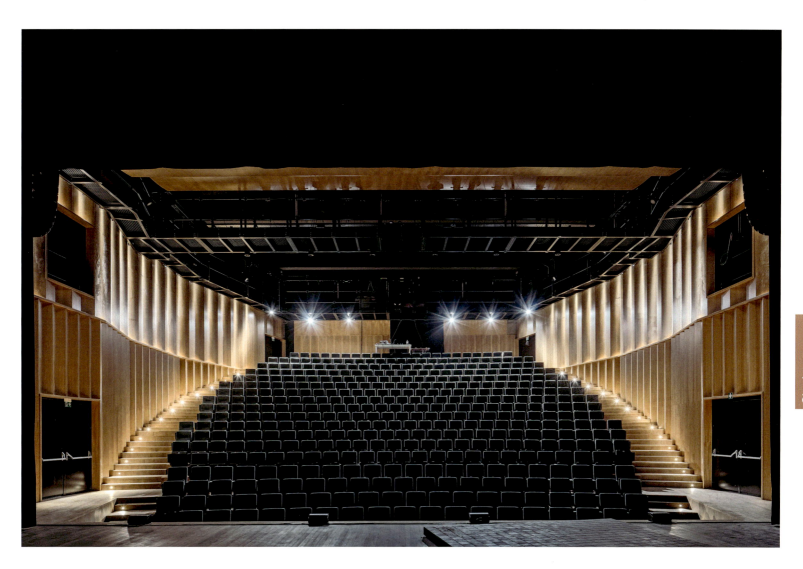

The theme of light and shadow, bright and dark, can also be found in the foyer.

A+R ARCHITEKTEN
Project Burma Hospital in Myanmar

Oliver Braun, Hellmut Raff, Florian Gruner, Alexander Lange and Walter Fritz

ARCHITECT/S
a + r Architekten GmbH, Stuttgart / Germany

LOCATION
Magyizin, Myanmar

BUILDING PURPOSE
Health

CONSTRUCTION PERIOD
2016–2019

BRICK TYPE
Facing bricks

On the remote Indian Ocean coast in southwest Myanmar lies the village of Magyizin, which, like its neighboring towns, is still characterized by an originality that at first glance seems idyllic. Traditional construction methods and a small-scale settlement structure predominate. This supposed naturalness has its price, of course: There is no paved road into the region and the existing dirt roads are not passable during the rainy season. The communities here also have no other connection to the infrastructure that we naturally expect, such as to the power grid or medical care. The non-profit aid organization Projekt Burma e.V. has set its sights on improving the living conditions of people affected by poverty and organizes aid projects for one of the world's poorest countries. The association has succeeded in building a hospital in Magyizin, financed exclusively by donations, in order to make medical care accessible to the residents more quickly. As a central hospital, it supplies 20 communities and around 20,000 people. The facility features 20 beds, an operating room, a delivery room, a laboratory, an instrument cleaning room and two separate patient rooms for infectious patients.

Situated on a hill and thus protected from tsunamis, the new building, whose typology and construction method were based on local traditions, was erected by the villagers under the guidance of a carpenter, as there are no construction companies in this region. The single-story main structure surrounds a weather-protected atrium from which the patient rooms, the treatment and staff rooms and the medicine dispensary are accessible. Connected to the main building via an arcade, the linear side wing accommodates the kitchen, the sanitary, washing and storage spaces, as well as the isolation ward.

> "The exposed bricks have a soothing effect on the hospital's patients."

Inspired by the country's typical "brick nogging structure," the new building was erected in a skeleton construction of reinforced concrete with brick infill. Two-tiered panels with wooden slats shade the openings; the lower tier can be positioned to control the light and air supply. Above this, an open frieze made of bamboo sticks ensures the constant circulation of air, which plays a significant role in construction in tropical climates. The underside of the roof structure made of timber trusses is mostly clad with woven bamboo mats through which the air flows and can be discharged again via ventilation louvres in ridge of the gable top.

The façade is characterized by a clear horizontal layering and a natural interaction of brick, wood, concrete and bamboo. Mint green doors for the patient rooms and interior walls plastered in typical local colors create a bright and trusting atmosphere. [ch]

Sharing public spaces

Project Burma Hospital in Myanmar

Lighting, ventilation and shading correspond to country-specific solutions.

ANTONIO VIRGA ARCHITECTE
Cinema Le Grand Palais

Antonio Virga

ARCHITECT/S
antonio virga architecte, Paris/France

LOCATION
Cahors, France

BUILDING PURPOSE
Leisure

CONSTRUCTION PERIOD
2018–2019

BRICK TYPE
Facing bricks, roof tiles

Early 20th century cinemas were often architecturally exceptional buildings, elaborately decorated with classical columns, exotic flora or modernist geometries and painted in opulent colors. A visit to these buildings — movie palaces, as they were called —, was an out-of-the-ordinary experience. Le Grand Palais in the town of Cahors in French Occitania evokes this glorious history of cinemas not only through its name. It was developed by the municipal administration and was part of a larger redevelopment of the urban area north from the town's historical center. The new movie theater building is placed between three- to four-story apartment buildings that once belonged to the military. The structure of the cinema reconstructs one wing in this strict-looking group of buildings and adds a new public function to the area. In order to house the large program of the multi-hall cinema, Le Grand Palais is made up of two adjacent, yet different volumes: a more public one finished with light sandstone-colored brick, and a slightly withdrawn second volume clad in golden aluminum panels.

Indoors, the building houses seven cinema halls in its four stories, with two large ones that can be entered from the ground floor and five smaller ones accessed from the third. Altogether, there are over one thousand seats in the cinema. Entrances to the separate halls are marked by deep blue niches and backlit numbers on their sides, preparing the viewer for the movie experience. The halls are finished equally in dark blue hues. The whitewashed entrance hall is illuminated by incident light falling laterally through the perforated brick walls and by the circular chandeliers.

> "Our office has consistently worked in the pursuit of a timeless contemporary architecture; an aesthetic that is both relevant to our time, and firmly rooted in history."

In the exterior, the narrow brick evokes associations with local building traditions, referencing the natural mud brick that is still seen in the town's medieval fortifications. Its continuous surface wraps the unarticulated volume into one whole. Yet, to avoid monotony, the façade changes its appearance on the second and third story levels, where the perforated surface provides light to the foyer space during the daytime and from where light glows out to the square in the evenings. The golden surface of the second volume is perforated with small, round openings, forming rhomboid patterns across its walls. The duality of the two volumes calls the viewer to reflect on the historical character and references to the past on the surfaces of the new building. Through its exotic light effects, Le Grand Palais refers to its function of a cinema as a play of light. Its abstract ornamentation in turn summons the glamor of historic movie palaces by referencing the abstract geometries of 1920s Art Deco. These summonings are like traces that indicate their meaning not through similarity or copying past forms, but through the use of contemporary means and materials. [ak]

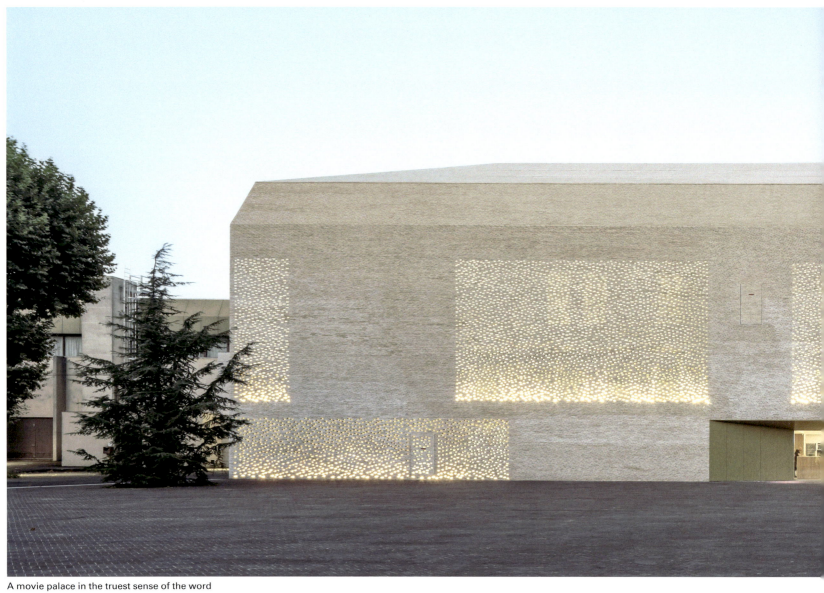
A movie palace in the truest sense of the word

Sharing public spaces

COLECTIVO C733
Matamoros Public Market

José Amozurrutia, Israel Espin, Eric Valdez, Gabriela Carillo and Carlos Facio

ARCHITECT/S
Colectivo C733, Mexico City / Mexico

LOCATION
Matamoros, Tamaulipas, Mexico

BUILDING PURPOSE
Infrastructure

CONSTRUCTION PERIOD
2019–2020

BRICK TYPE
Clay blocks

Markets in Mexico have always been important public places of great commercial and cultural significance. This fact even impressed the Spanish conquistador Hernán Cortés: "The city has many open squares in which markets are continuously held…," he wrote in 1521. "One square in particular is twice as big as that of Salamanca and completely surrounded by arcades where there are daily more than sixty thousand folks buying and selling."

> "The use of inner patios, local materials, crossed ventilation, orientation and façade density to protect from direct sunlight are some of the building's principal characteristics."

In 2019, the Architecture Faculty of the National Autonomous University of Mexico launched a competition for the design of a reproducible market building on behalf of the Ministry of Agrarian, Territorial and Urban Development. It chose a socially problematic district of Matamoros, a city in northeast Mexico right on the border with the United States, as the location. The task was to design an affordable structure that could also be completed in just three months. The winning design originates from a project team called C733, formed under the direction of Gabriela Carillo with four other architects. They developed a market building whose patio typology refers to Native American as well as Spanish and Arabic traditions.

The construction consists essentially of metal profiles and masonry made of clay blocks. Its division is based on a basic grid of 12×21 square modules, each 3×3 meters in size, enclosed on all sides by a brick wall with ten visitor entrances. Forty fixed market stalls separated by partitions line the wall on the inside. The service area and storage rooms are located at the southern end of the building, where a delivery entrance can also be found.

A half-covered area with 40 3×3-meter spaces for temporary market stalls opens up between the fixed stands. They are situated under a roof structure made of large, trapezoidal funnels that stand on 12-centimeter-thick metal supports. To provide for heat insulation and rainwater drainage, the funnels are filled with two-centimeter-thick clay bricks and the top is covered with corrugated sheet metal. The collected rainwater is used to water a garden with native plants, which forms the heart of the market.

The umbrella-like construction is reminiscent of the market opened in Coyoacán, Mexico in 1956, designed by Félix Candela and Pedro Ramírez Vázquez. While this forerunner features an exposed concrete structure, the Matamoros Public Market is deliberately designed to be very light and flexible. To enable the building to be reproduced in other locations, it consists of prefabricated parts, combined with materials such as clay bricks laid on site by local craftsmen, which can be changed depending on the location. Its structure is also flexible, so that the function can change if necessary. Its main goal, after all, is to create a place for social exchange, similar to the pre-Hispanic markets. [ab]

Sharing public spaces

Matamoros Public Market

The simple and modular structure allows the hall to be reproduced in different sizes and with flexible uses.

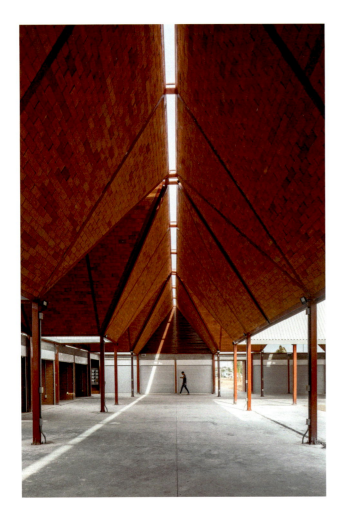

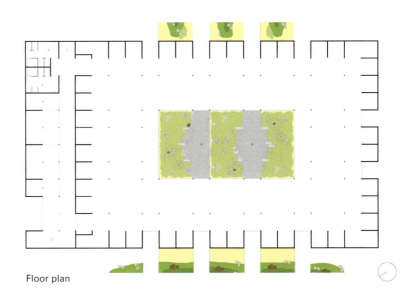

Floor plan

Sharing public spaces

203

BRENAC & GONZALEZ & ASSOCIÉS
Rosa Parks School

Guillaume Marechaux, Olivier Brenac, Emmanuel Person, Xavier Gonzalez and Jean-Pierre Leveque

ARCHITECT/S
Brenac & Gonzalez & Associés, Paris / France

LOCATION
Villeurbanne, France

BUILDING PURPOSE
Education

CONSTRUCTION PERIOD
2018–2019

BRICK TYPE
Facing bricks

Villeurbanne is a city just west of Lyon. It is known to architecture fans for the Cité de gratte-ciel, built in the early 1930s, a city center with a town hall at the end of an axial complex, which combines elements of modernist architecture with those of the Beaux Arts tradition and stands out from the urban fabric though a gleaming whiteness.

> "Hand-molded, glazed, forming a mashrabiya, the brick shows its multiple facets in Villeurbanne."

Just a few meters north of this is the site on which the new Rosa Parks preschool and elementary school were erected up until 2019. Industrial and commercial buildings, as well as typical large-sized residential structures from the post-war period and several older ones, characterize the immediate vicinity. An urban redevelopment program will give the area west of the school a new face. In this context, the new complex is intended as a connecting joint between the adjacent areas. It closes the block development with an L-shaped figure and is staggered in height so that the corner is prominently articulated and the courtyard and the building sides facing it receive sufficient sunlight. Since the property offered little space for outdoor facilities, the architects designed the volume to create a veritable roof landscape that the pupils can use. White metal structures frame the free spaces on the upper floors with metal mesh so that they are suitable for children to play without restricting them. A stepped field of open and closed, free and covered areas, and relationships between the levels unfolds.

The brick chosen as the façade material plays a vital role. With a pattern of sand-colored and white bricks, it enriches the variety of space and light situations and ties in with the white buildings of the Cité de gratte-ciel. The matt white, glazed bricks are interspersed in the masonry bonds like points of light. This play with the different permeable surfaces is enhanced by areas where the bricks were placed in gaps. The result is a translucent lattice pattern that turns walls into membranes between inside and outside. At the same time, the brick and the finely graduated light hues ensure that the building is perceived as an entity. The lattice motifs are also used on the façades facing the streets above the glazed ground floor protected by metal lamellas: Here the gradations between inside and outside are more reserved, without being completely withdrawn. In addition to loggias, the perforated masonry walls show where the open areas are — with the appropriate time of day and lighting, they appear as shimmering fields. This richly varied play is complemented by the impressive staircase in the "corner tower" that connects all floors, giving it an internal and functional correspondence. [ch]

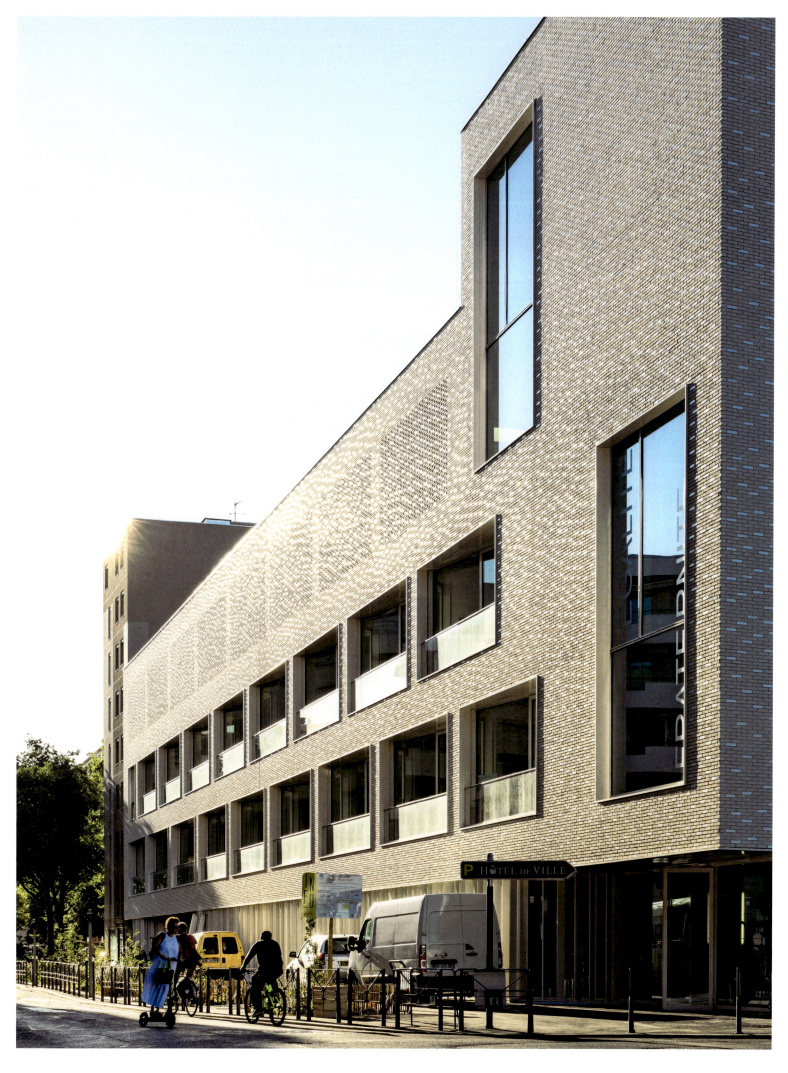

Rosa Parks School

The lively roof landscape and wide arcades serve as relaxation and play areas for the children.

MAGÉN ARQUITECTOS
Auditorium-Theatre in the Old Quarter of Illueca

Jaime Magén and Francisco Javier Magén

ARCHITECT/S
MAGÉN ARQUITECTOS
Zaragoza / Spain

LOCATION
Illueca, Spain

BUILDING PURPOSE
Culture

CONSTRUCTION PERIOD
2018–2020

BRICK TYPE
Facing bricks

Illueca is located west of Zaragoza in northeastern Spain. The small town is impressively dominated by a castle. The urban fabric presses tightly against the castle hill. Illueca has recently added another attraction — and in contrast to the castle, which is largely used as a hotel, it is one for the local population. Not only is the new cultural building for a little more than 200 visitors an attraction as a performance venue, the careful and skillful way in which it interweaves with the existing structure also makes it a special place. To counteract an impending population decline, the town council decided to erect it in place of an old cinema. The design according to which the theater was built was the result of a competition.

> "In a small town, the vibrant ceramic volumes blend the auditorium with its context."

The building appears to be made up of several houses with flat sloping roofs, houses like those found all over the city. These supposed four houses that make up the theater are not an arbitrary composition, because a functional area is under each of the four roofs: a stage tower, auditorium, foyer and a service area with cloakrooms and restrooms. This division also enables the architects to react to the slope and to cope with a height difference of 2.5 meters. Incisions have been made in several places — a covered entrance area is created, the high stage tower is separated from the foyer in the street view, and the stage access is identified.

The building is characterized by just a few materials. Especially outside, but also in the foyer, bricks determine the surfaces. Concrete, wood, glass and a few white plastered walls also ensure that a balance between the effect of space and material is maintained. Here, too, the assignment follows a clear concept, because each material is clearly related to a specific function: exposed concrete to the load-bearing horizontal surfaces; wood to the windows, doors and fixtures; bricks to the outer walls and the internal walls from the auditorium to the foyer. In the outdoor area, a dark red natural stone base provides a visual foundation. The red brick picks up on color and material moods from the surroundings and continues them inside, evoking the local pottery tradition as well. Outside and inside, the surfaces vary and ensure an exciting interplay of differently designed surfaces. Bricks placed on gaps create lattice structures that filter the light. Inside the building, perforated bricks are laid to make them acoustically effective and to add a further component to the interplay of various surfaces.

What ultimately emerged was an architectural jewel that foregoes exaggerated or spectacular gestures and does not have to celebrate the new, but rather relies entirely on the sensitive updating of the existing. [ch]

Auditorium-Theatre in the Old Quarter of Illueca

To correspond to the small-scaled structure of the neighborhood, the house appears as four parts.

Sharing public spaces

B-ARCHITECTEN & BEVK PEROVIĆ ARHITEKTI
Erasmus University College

Sven Grooten, Evert Crols and Dirk Engelen   Vasa Perović and Matija Bevk

ARCHITECT/S
B-architecten, Antwerp/Belgium;
Bevk Perović Arhitekti, Lubljana/Slovenia

LOCATION
Brussels, Belgium

BUILDING PURPOSE
Education

CONSTRUCTION PERIOD
2017–2020

BRICK TYPE
Clay blocks, facing bricks, reused bricks

The new campus building of the Erasmus University of Applied Sciences and Arts in Brussels is situated in the vibrant Dansaert district of the central city, a few steps away from the Brussels canal. Intended for over one thousand students, it provides space for the departments of teacher training and pedagogy, as well as tourism and recreation management classes. On its western side, the brick and glass building is extended by a historic red-brick warehouse of a former brewery, the two parts being joined together by a tall stairwell that, on the outside, is clad with perforated aluminum panels. In this way, for an onlooker from the street, the building offers an interplay of solid masses and transparencies, of surfaces with different textures and character being juxtaposed in the manner of minimal art. But it also draws our attention to urban continuities, the ways in which functions need to be fitted to pre-existing configurations, and how the new forms in turn contribute to previous historical layers.

Indoors, the transparent ground floor with glass walls opening to the surrounding streets includes a library, a large study area, and a cafeteria that extends to an open-air terrace. Contrary to the indoor spaces, the terrace is separated from the street by a two-story high latticed wall, repeating the aluminum panels of the staircase on the ground level and the perforated brick bond above it. There are two underground floors with spacious auditoria on both of them. The central staircase that functions also as a light shaft between the two parts of the building leads to the upper floors with special subjects classrooms (including classes for future hairdressers and beauty salon workers) and teachers' rooms. On the top floor is a spacious meeting room for the staff. Adhering to contemporary sustainability standards, the building has weather-controlled heating systems, ventilation with heat recovery providing all rooms with fresh air, a system collecting rainwater for the building's use and solar panels on the roof. Moreover, the bricks from the demolished smaller structures on the site were recycled and re-used for the renovation of the brewery building: The new, lighter stones on its walls now form random patterns against the original, darker red-brick background.

> "The use of brickwork was key to unifying the character of the old warehouse and the new campus."

It is a building of surfaces, layers and connections: The façade of the main volume is dominated by the large, dark brick wall oriented to the triangular square in front of the building; on the sides, all-glass walls bring light to its classrooms, the aluminum-clad staircase mediates the encounter between the new and old parts, providing a neutral link between the darker and lighter brick surfaces. Inside, perforated wooden panels covering the classroom walls intersperse with unobstructed views through the floor-to-ceiling windows and the low vaulting of the concrete ceilings in the older part of the building. The visible difference of the materials, underscored by their contrasting juxtaposition, makes you want to run your fingers across the unique surfaces and literally touch the building. But the connections function also on a more abstract level: If the former warehouse brings to mind the industrial past of the area and its profitable brewery trade, the school training people for work in tourism and pedagogy tells of the dominant business model in the present, when hospitality and education form a large share in the cities' income. [ak]

The aluminum-clad stair tower connects the two parts of the building.

Erasmus University College

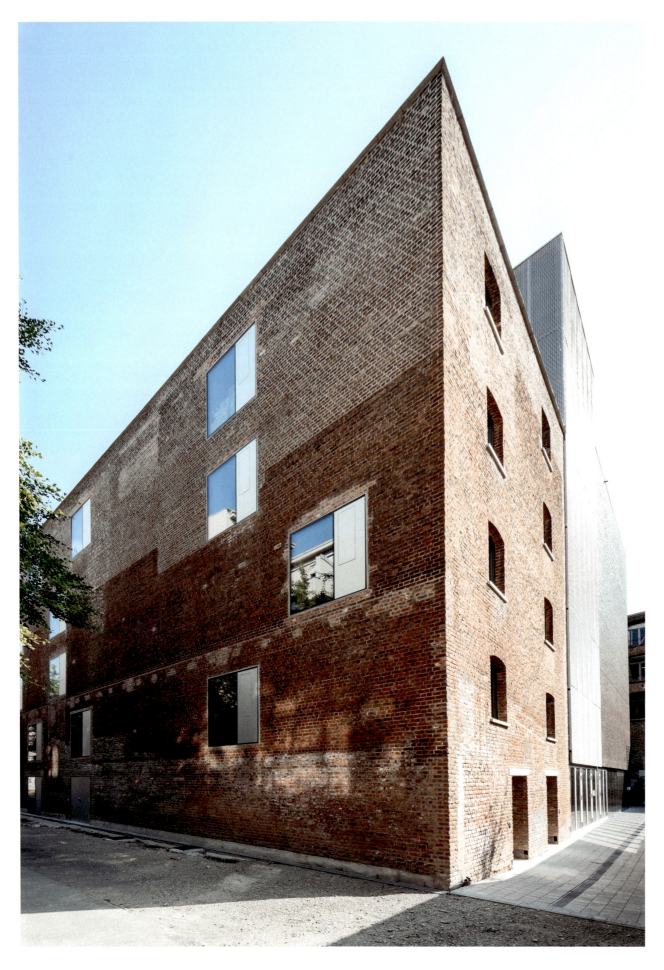

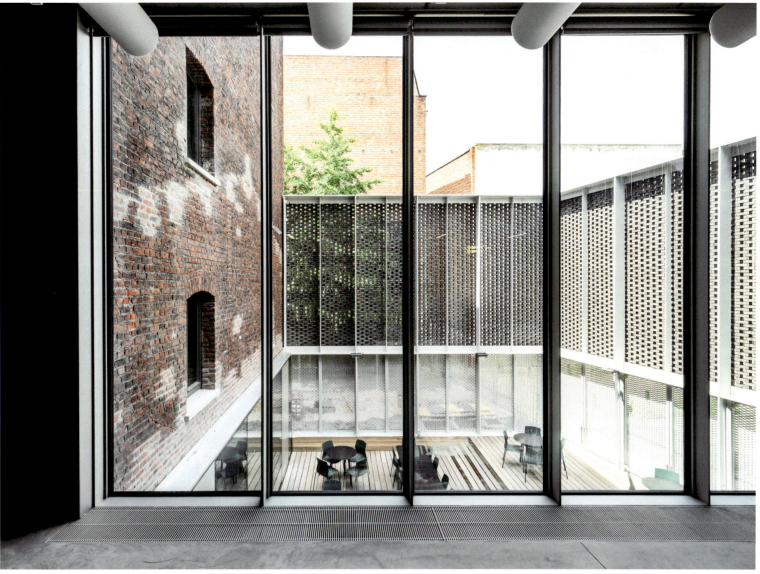

The interplay of surfaces and textures can also be found in the terrace area.

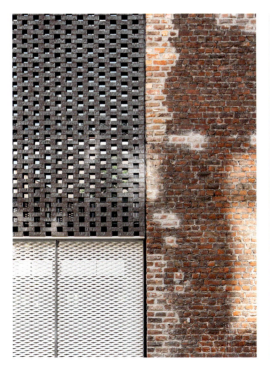

ZERO ENERGY DESIGN LAB ARCHITECTS
Girls' Hostel Block, St. Andrews Institute of Technology and Management

Sachin Rastogi and Payal Seth Rastogi

ARCHITECT/S
Zero Energy Design Lab Architects, New Delhi/India

LOCATION
Gurugram, India

BUILDING PURPOSE
Student hostel

CONSTRUCTION PERIOD
2016–2020

BRICK TYPE
Facing bricks

Founded in 2012, the St. Andrews Institute of Technology and Management is located in the greater New Delhi area. Since the pupils live on site, a hostel block for the girls was completed for the institute in 2020 right next to the one for the boys — as a building that combines simplicity and clarity with sophistication.

> "The building unfolds as a series of multidimensional sequence of spaces through the method of adaptive layering which gives rise to 'sustainability as a way of living.'"

The functional structure is lucid and coherent. The floor plans of the four-story house are organized as a two-tier structure, with the girls' rooms to the right and left of the central corridor, with their own balconies. A glazed foyer that opens across two floors and is crowned by a generously cantilevered terrace adorns the building's front.

What is special about the structure, however, is its staircase and the outer shell, which act as an important factor in the climate concept. They are placed in front of the building in the south and extend over its entire length. The direction of the stairs bends horizontally from floor to floor, giving it a light and unconstrained look. The path leads from the stairs into the house over widening bridges and corridors. Since these are amply dimensioned, they also serve as lounge areas and communication points.

From the second floor onwards, the staircase is overlaid with an open, porous skin: A skeletal structure made of concrete, into which the course of the stairs is woven, is covered with a "network" of open, slightly rotated hollow blocks made of red-colored concrete. Using a parametric method, the arrangement of the blocks was optimized so that they absorb as much heat as possible while providing good light transmission. This means that the circulation path is not only the hinge between inside and outside, but also a buffer zone, which helps to ensure that the actual façade does not heat up as much — this reduces the cooling load by 35 percent. On the north side, the same double-skin layer method is used to cool the incoming air.

The inner façade is made of bricks, a traditional, inexpensive and easily available building material familiar to craftsmen. They appear on the outside on the balustrades of the terrace and balconies as well as on the front sides of the building. As an expressive element, the outer skin — especially on the south side — is the building's calling card, but it is only when the bricks are used in a variety of ways that a lively image of different textures emerges. [ch]

Sharing public spaces

Girls' Hostel Block, St. Andrews Institute of Technology and Management

The access layer placed in front of the building is part of the climate concept.

Sharing public spaces

UMARCHITEKT, ULRICH MANZ WITH M. KUNTZ AND CH. GATZ
Jewish Museum Franconia

Ulrich Manz

ARCHITECT/S
umarchitekt
Ulrich Manz with
M. Kuntz and Ch. Gatz,
Bamberg/Germany

LOCATION
Fürth, Germany

BUILDING PURPOSE
Museum

CONSTRUCTION PERIOD
2015–2018

BRICK TYPE
Facing bricks

Regarded as one of the most important institutions of its kind in Germany, the Jewish Museum Franconia imparts the long history of Jewish life in this region—at three locations (Fürth, Schnaittach and Schwabach). In 2008, a competition aimed at further opening the museum to the public and creating spaces for events and special exhibitions was announced. A special library, a café, a museum shop and administrative rooms were to additionally expand the existing structure.

The Gatz, Kuntz + Manz consortium's winning design was realized. Not only did the architects succeed in organizing the desired spatial program in a compact structure in a richly exciting way, they also integrated the museum, despite the decidedly contemporary architectural language, into the context of the historical development.

The ground floor with the new entrance, shop and café attaches to the base of the existing building and encloses a small courtyard in the interstice between the old and the new structures. Towards the other side, a floor-to-ceiling window connects the event hall with the small square in front of the annex. From this vantage point one can also see how the building volume has been stepped backwards to make it fit well with the historical structure. The windows on the upper floors are set so that they arouse curiosity without completely revealing the interior. This is where the library, administrative spaces, internal staff rooms and a storage depot are housed. A corridor runs between the old and the new on the top floor. Two-story areas link the floors and create exciting spatial sequences, while the basement provides space for temporary exhibitions.

> "I like the idea that a natural material made of baked earth can be used to create a wide variety of atmospheres in a sustainable way."

As the new solitaire in the series of existing buildings, the extension is not only accentuated by its concise shape, but also by its warm, light dress, which, as a back-ventilated façade, surrounds the solid construction with bricks. Its surfaces are richly varied as well. The rustica masonry of the old building plinth rhythmically continues in the base area, for instance, through a series of sharp-edged, slanted vertical strips. Perforated sunshade panels have been placed in front of several windows. On the upper floors, the façade is structured by bricks slightly twisted out of the surface and, depending on the incidence of light, sometimes leave a soft impression, other times an angular one. An ocher-colored slurry applied to the clinkers nearly makes the joint pattern disappear but emphasizes the plasticity of the surface all the more. It lends the new building a jewel case-like character that is resistant on the outside and holds valuable items inside. [ch]

Sharing public spaces

Jewish Museum Franconia

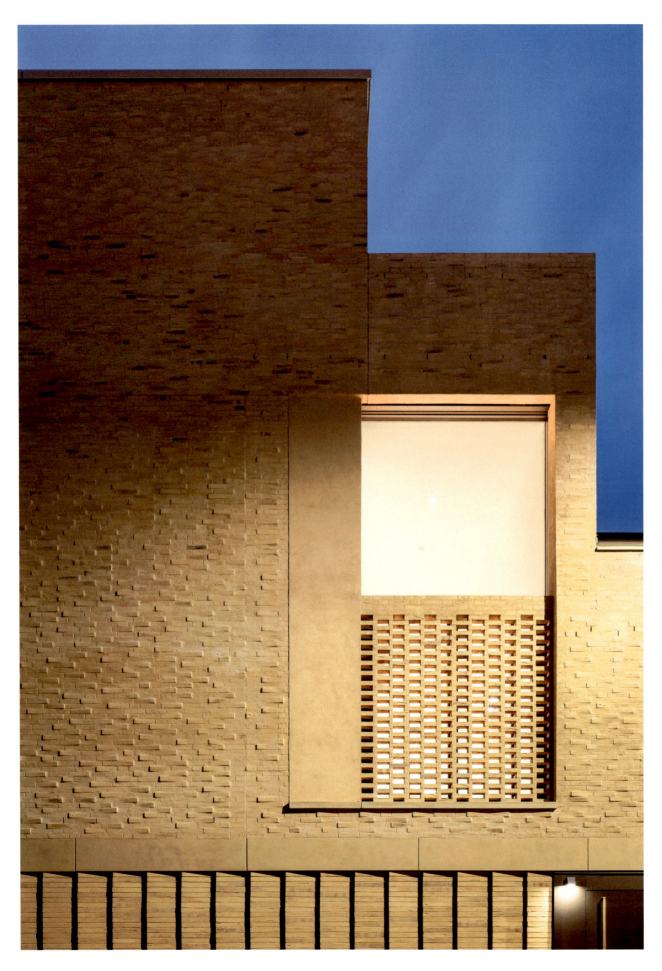

Site plan

The contrasting height gradation creates the transition between old and new.

Sharing public spaces

DOMINIQUE COULON & ASSOCIÉS
Housing for the Elderly in Huningue

Dominique Coulon

ARCHITECT/S
Dominique Coulon & associés, Strasbourg/France

LOCATION
Huningue, France

BUILDING PURPOSE
Residential housing

CONSTRUCTION PERIOD
2016–2018

BRICK TYPE
Facings bricks, craft bricks

This two-story building is situated on the banks of the river Rhine, in the small town of Huningue in southeastern France, a spot where the country meets up with Switzerland and Germany. The low all-brick volume has large square windows connected with horizontal bands and slanting surfaces between them, blurring any direct typological associations and placing itself between the public and the private functions. This position is intentional. The house has twenty-two independent apartments for the elderly on both floors and shared common rooms—like a canteen, the multimedia room and the workshop rooms—on the ground floor. Collective activities are encouraged for the inhabitants, but at the same time the house has to allow for seclusion if needed. This delicate separation between the public and the private zones is continued with the entrances to the individual apartments that remain at first hidden from sight when one steps into the house directly from the street. It is a carefully choreographed play of looks and movement inside the house.

The focal point for the public areas is the main staircase, standing in the middle of the H-shaped plan of the ground floor and lit by a large window suspended over the main hall on the second floor. On the landing is a built-in wooden bench, allowing for resting and casual conversations. The pink concrete of the interior walls and the terracotta paving of the floors in the central core change to wooden flooring and white walls in the dining areas, with the fireplace of green glazed tiles and similar flooring around it adding an element of coziness. The materials and architectural elements speak here through metaphors and allegory, rather than direct symbols, generating associations and connection points for inhabitants with different life trajectories. The individual units of 50 square meters in size provide an open kitchen with a dining and living area, a bathroom and a sleeping alcove. Ventilation is provided through shutters in the window bay, covered on the outside with a lattice brickwork wall.

"By emphasizing its rustic port setting, the building connects itself to the history of the Rhine."

The project by architect Dominique Coulon was carried out according to a winning entry in a competition in 2013 that was organized by the local municipality. Referencing regional building traditions, the house was finished with artisanal brick that is occasionally non-standard and irregular, alluding to its craft character and offering an attractive haptic texture. This roughness of the stone surfaces is contrasted with the maximal attention to detailing and building quality, with its seamless glazing of the windows and projecting stretchers that adds texture to the outer wall surfaces. With its unusual attention to materials and spatial structures, this is a building that is at the forefront of offering new ways for living together in an older age, of inventing new typologies of care. [ak]

Housing for the Elderly in Huningue

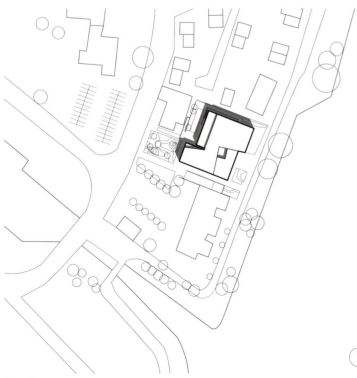

Site plan

The common areas are oriented to the Rhine.

Building outside the box

230 WOJCIECH CZAJA
One Building Block of Many:
A Call to Play and Experiment

234 NERI&HU DESIGN AND RESEARCH OFFICE
The Brick Wall — Tsingpu
Yangzhou Retreat

242 GRAMAZIO KOHLER RESEARCH, ETH ZURICH;
INCON.AI; ROB TECHNOLOGIES AG,
ZURICH/SWITZERLAND
Augmented Bricklaying

246 BERGER+PARKKINEN ASSOCIATED ARCHITECTS
Paracelsus Bad & Kurhaus

250 WALLMAKERS
Pirouette House

254 BODENSTEINER FEST ARCHITECTS
Casa Rossa Chemnitz

258 BANGKOK PROJECT STUDIO
The Elephant World :
Non-Human-Centered Architecture

262 HARQUITECTES
Clos Pachem Winery

266 CTA | CREATIVE ARCHITECTS
Wall House

270 MONADNOCK & DE ZWARTE HOND
Park Pavilion

WOJCIECH CZAJA
One Building Block of Many: A Call to Play and Experiment

Wojciech Czaja

Ferry in 't Veld, 37 years old, an architect by trade, as well something like an exploratory spirit who looks beyond the edge of the screen and builds outside of his own box, stands on Gouvernestraat in the Rotterdam city center in front of his house, a beautiful but inconspicuous structure at first glance, and strokes the ocher brick wall with his hand. "Do you see the small, white, shiny particles embedded in the surface? Now guess what that is!"

He developed the caramel-colored brick together with his partner Nina Aalbers, and shaped and fired it a thousand times with a local producer in the north of Holland. The focus of this not quite everyday undertaking was on the topic of recycling and the circular economy. And, well, one of the largest mountains of rubble that grows skyward year after year during renovation and demolition work consists of old washbasins, toilets and urinals broken into pieces. Almost 23 tons of it now carve out a life after sanitary death in in 't Veld's walls.

"Shocking, isn't it? But somehow also wonderfully poetic when one considers the beauty that can be produced from waste." In contrast to conventional bricks, the recycled brick in in 't Veld's house is only 30 percent clay. The remaining 70 percent is ceramic rubble and glass. The latter melts during the firing process, liquefies and mutates at around 800 degrees Celsius to become a binding agent for the mélange of building waste collected all around. "That is exactly what fascinates me about this building material. The brick is never thought through to the end but is constantly evolving. And who knows which additives we will be including tomorrow or the day after tomorrow!"

Not only in Rotterdam, the brick is a catalyst for progress and building culture development worldwide. Several parameters such as clay, fire and manageable size are fixed constants and have remained nearly unchanged for centuries and millennia. However, other properties — such as soil quality, additives, geometry, firing temperature and, not least, the architectural composition on site — are subject to permanent, never boring change. Even more, due to its compact dimensions and its associated low weight, what is undoubtedly the most democratic of all building materials encourages chemical, physical and constructive experimentation.

One of the most breathtaking examples of the formal and constructive diversity of the brick that I have ever set eyes (as well as all other sensory perceptions) on is the Bagan temple complex, picturesquely situated in the Irrawaddy Valley in the heartland of Myanmar. The oldest terracotta structures date back to the 10th and 11th centuries, and if one touches the surface of the Nanpaya Temple, the Nathlaung Kyaung Temple or the 41-meter-high Shwesandaw Pagoda like Ferry in 't Veld, then it feels as if brownies had rightly sculpted soul houses for Buddhist celestial giants in precision work. The beauty shaped, carved, fired and laid here in various bonds is evidence of the joy of and suitability for experimentation that brick provides as a building material. Of the 10,000 temples once erected in Bagan, more than 2,200 have been preserved to this day — even though the area was only placed under protection as a UNESCO World Heritage Site three years ago.

Even in the recent past, brick has repeatedly been an incentive for top architectural achievements. At the Kantana Film and Animation Institute in Nakhon Pathom Province, a training center for filmmakers and animation artists in the west of Bangkok, the outside walls dance samba. Made of 600,000 handcrafted bricks that tower up to eight meters into the sky, the bulging walls seem to set the building in motion. Concealed behind the visual sensuality of the architect Boonserm Premthada is a low-tech machine in terms of building physics: Since the bricks partially shade themselves, the wall remains pleasantly cool. Thanks to its hollow interior and the high storage capacity, the structure works like an upside-down fireplace. The air contained in the space between the walls cools down, falls downwards, becomes part of a branched air chamber system in the foundation and in this way supplies the entire campus with fresh air at the right temperature. There is no simpler or cheaper way to build an air conditioning system.

Further highlights—all located in the rural Global South and proof that ingenuity is not necessarily a question of financial resources, but in most cases is born out of a lack, out of an inner longing for the optimum—include the Terra Cotta Studio in Quang Nam, Central Vietnam (Tropical Space Architects), the Sai Mandir Hindu temple in Vennached, India (SEA Studio) and the Maya Somaiya Library in Kopargaon, likewise India, where Sameep Padora & Associates succeeded in wresting the gravity from a wafer-thin, just ten-centimeter-thick and more than five-hundred-square-meter-large brick shell, stretching it into a pillarless, walkable dome. Goose bumps.

This year's nominations in the "Building outside the box" category are part of exactly this culture of permanent reinvention: The Paracelsus Bad & Kurhaus in Salzburg stands—as in Rotterdam—for the development of a new material. The Casa Rossa in Chemnitz is—as in Bagan—a symbol for the longevity and aging ability of the building material. And the Wall House in Bien Hoa, the Pirouette House in Trivandrum and the Kitrus Winery near Thessaloniki, whose wonderfully moving façade was developed by ETH Zurich using laser technology and an augmented reality interface, make the constructive, geometric and design potentials in this millennia-old building material visible in an impressive way.

One of the strongest and most touching projects, however, is Elephant World in Surin, Thailand. With few means, but all the more humility and sensitivity, a habitat for humans and animals was created that unites the oft-contradicting qualities inherent in the material: grace and mass, lightness and eternity, playfulness and unshakable archaism. In addition to the poetic labyrinth, a proverbial lighthouse marks the importance of this never-constant material culture.

In the years and decades to come, the need to think out of the box and expand it will continue to grow. Political, economic and health crises, on the one hand, the threatening and undiminishing consequences of the climate crisis, on the other hand, open up a wide field of activity for architecture, urban planning, regional development, industry and infrastructure. The specific tasks are set out in at least six of the 17 Sustainable Development Goals of the United Nations. The brick will not be able to master all of these tasks. But in the right hands of creative thinkers, it is one building block of many.

NERI&HU DESIGN AND RESEARCH OFFICE
The Brick Wall — Tsingpu Yangzhou Retreat

Lyndon Neri and Rossana Hu

ARCHITECT/S
Neri&Hu Design and Research Office, Shanghai/China

LOCATION
Yangzhou, China

BUILDING PURPOSE
Hotel

CONSTRUCTION PERIOD
2018

BRICK TYPE
Facing bricks, roof tiles, paving bricks

BRICK 22 Category Winner

Part of an artificial lake landscape near the Chinese city of Yanghzou, Silver Lake attracts many tourists every year. A new boutique hotel with 20 rooms was to be built on a 32,000-square-meter-large site on the lakeshore. However, the area was not a tabula rasa, but contained an old warehouse and several small houses where farmers and fishermen had previously lived.

> "Neri&Hu utilizes a landscape to unify a complex site and program, while the rustic materiality and layered spaces seek to redefine tradition with a modern architectural language."

At the request of the client, the existing buildings were to be at least partially retained and serve as identity-establishing elements. The question of how to reconcile a luxury hotel and a handful of modest cottages scattered all over the property then arose. Neri&Hu found the solution in the typology of traditional Chinese courtyard houses. They laid a grid over the site that integrates the existing buildings. The result — to try to make a non-Chinese comparison — was a casbah-like structure of brick-walled paths and courtyards, which ensures hierarchy and arrangement. With the exception of a two-story courtyard house where the library and several guest rooms are located, all buildings within the grid are single-story. This turns the hotel into a labyrinth that does not reveal its secrets at first glance and wants to be discovered by the visitor.

The "brick walls" embrace all functional areas, which also include four gardens: a bamboo, a flower, a tea and a water garden. They consist partly of closed, partly of open masonry, and in some places the heads of every second brick protrude from the wall, creating varied textures. Openings in the wall repeatedly offer views into individual patios.

Each patio is assigned a use: as a reception, restaurant or guest room. The buildings stand as separate pavilions in the courtyards so that outside space remains around them. Outside the patio grid there is an additional pavilion with four rooms on the lake shore. Situated at the northern end of the property is an old warehouse, in which the architects have accommodated a theater, exhibition spaces and a further restaurant.

All walls and floors are made of greenish-gray, uneven bricks. They are — in the sense of circular construction — reused bricks, most of which come from the immediate vicinity of the facility. Together with the integration of the existing structures, they give the hotel a sense of location, history, but above all a little roughness and a lot of patina, which forms an effective contrast to the luxurious hotel interior. [ab]

Existing buildings were integrated into the complex.

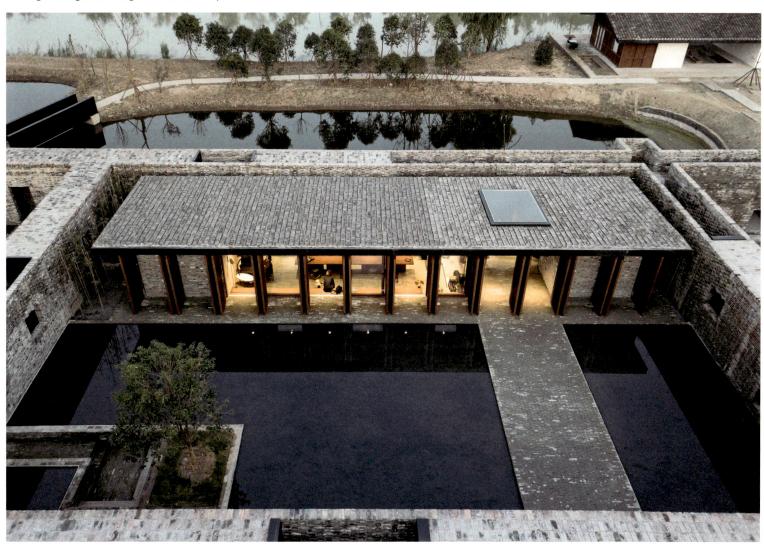

Building outside the box

235

The Brick Wall — Tsingpu Yangzhou Retreat

Jury Statement

"This remarkable project begins by reusing existing buildings and salvaging 1.2 million reclaimed local bricks to realize the Tsingpu Yangzhou Retreat. The rigorous plan is demarcated by a grid of gray brick walls and pathways that result in a series of distinctive open-air courtyards. Long perspective views down the interior brick passageways contrast with lyrical outdoor courtyards. These urban courtyard rooms are constantly blurring the boundaries between inside and out. Light animates the varied and unexpected brick patterns embedded in the project's masonry walls. Movement through the retreat reveals astonishing layered spaces and choreographed views of internal and external landscapes always linking earth and sky. The jury awards this project, as it emerges from the traditional architecture of the region and asserts a strong ethical commitment to sustainability and environmental responsibility by reusing and recycling."

The Brick Wall — Tsingpu Yangzhou Retreat

"Water Garden"

Connecting element is a grid of brick walls and paths.

Building outside the box

GRAMAZIO KOHLER RESEARCH, ETH ZURICH; INCON.AI; ROB TECHNOLOGIES AG, ZURICH / SWITZERLAND

Augmented Bricklaying

Kathrin Dörfler, Fabio Gramazio, Timothy Sandy, Daniela Mitterberger, Matthias Kohler and Foteini Salveridou

ARCHITECT/S
Gramazio Kohler Research, ETH Zurich; incon.ai; ROB Technologies AG, Zurich / Switzerland

LOCATION
Pydna, Greece

BUILDING PURPOSE
Winery

CONSTRUCTION PERIOD
2015–2018

BRICK TYPE
Facing bricks

Long known for its outstanding research in the realm of computer-aided construction methods, the Gramazio Kohler Research team made what was for many a surprising turn in its strategy for a Greek winery: The architects did not try to further replace human skills, but to specifically include them in the construction process.

Erected at the foot of Mount Olympus, the winery consists of a simple steel frame structure that serves to process and store wine. The façade panels of the construction were filled with brickwork. To ensure that the inside is always ventilated and one can still see clearly despite the subdued light, a façade that leaves gaps between the bricks was designed.

Most of all, however, they were searching for a way to implement a parametric façade design. Despite all the successes, it has become apparent that the deployment of robots is reaching its limits. On the one hand, there is the restricted mobility and dexterity of the robot arm; on the other hand, there is a particularly tight framework for handling formable material such as mortar. Instead of adapting the design to these constraints, an attempt was made here to shift them with the help of manual techniques and experience, as well as computer-aided methods. A pattern reminiscent of a surface of a wheat field swayed by the wind was developed. To create this effect, the mortar joints must vary, because only then can the bricks be individually rotated not only horizontally, but also vertically. Therefore, high craftsmanship is demanded here.

> "The varying mortar height allows the brick façade to playfully engage with the environment."

A tailor-made augmented reality user interface provides the bricklayers with immediately understandable information about how to lay the bricks. The placed brick can be fed back to the model via a camera and its position can then be specified more precisely. The accuracy and quality achieved in this way exceed the conventional holographic representations that are considered state-of-the art in this area. But not only was one technology surpassed by the other here. It was shown what potential lies in taking into account a building material often regarded as secondary, such as mortar in this case. And it was shown that the question of future building should be about recognizing the outstanding skills of people and using craft traditions so that they survive. Because if one integrates these into the construction process, one will be better off than if one does without them. [ch]

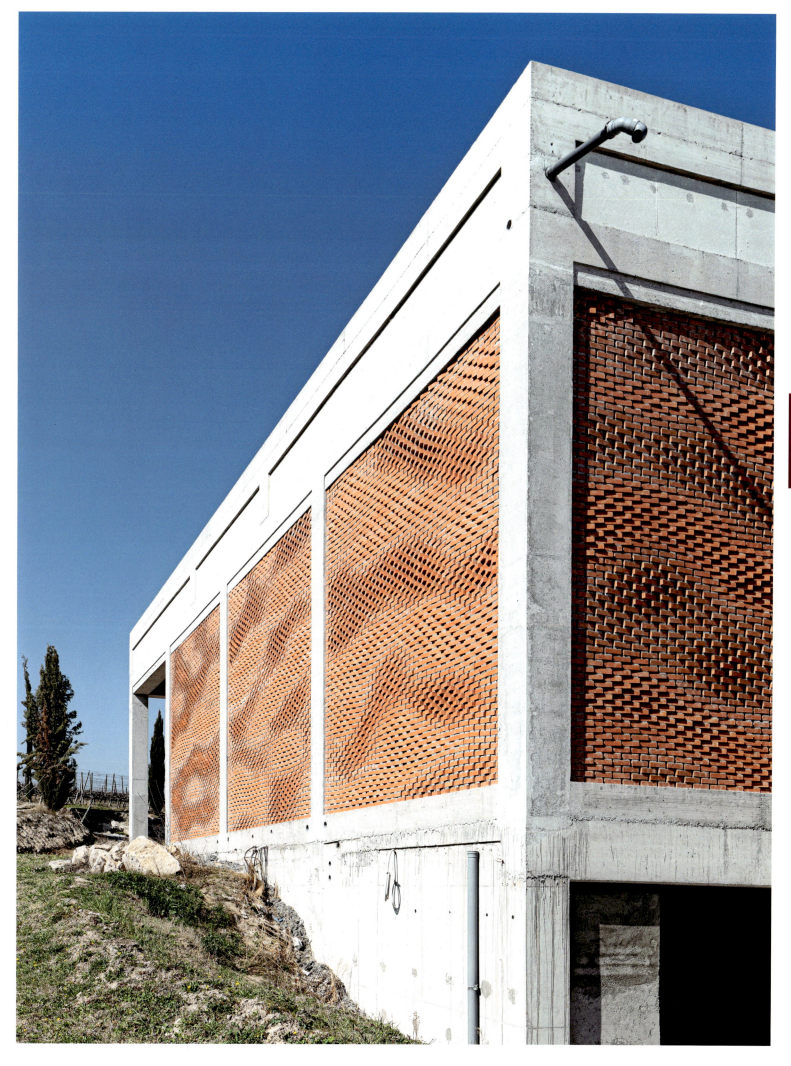

Building outside the box

Augmented Bricklaying

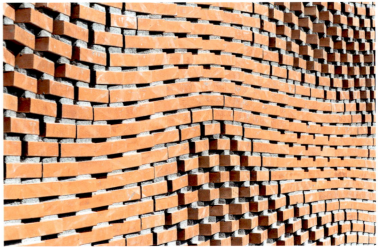

Building outside the box

BERGER+PARKKINEN ASSOCIATED ARCHITECTS
Paracelsus Bad & Kurhaus

Alfred Berger and Tina Parkkinen

ARCHITECT/S
Berger+Parkkinen
Associated Architects,
Vienna/Austria

LOCATION
Salzburg, Austria

BUILDING PURPOSE
Leisure, health

CONSTRUCTION PERIOD
2017–2019

BRICK TYPE
Ceramic façade panels

Swimming pools in urban settings have a long history, extending from simple brick reservoirs for ritual purification in ancient Indus Valley civilization to lavishly decorated bath complexes in imperial Rome. After the Industrial Revolution and the rapid growth in urban population, pools became sites for hygiene and exercise, as well as socializing and leisure, with quickly evolving typologies. Elegant, top-lit Art Deco bathing houses with colorful, glazed-tile walls provided space for relaxation and withdrawal from daily routine. Spacious swimming facilities, enabled by ferro-concrete beams and arches, offered larger spans for training and physical activity. The Paracelsus swimming pool and spa in Salzburg represents the preferences of the 21st century, combining leisure and care for the body with exercise and relaxation, in a sculptural and sustainable architectural framework.

> "Cladding the façade with a dress of glazed ceramic lamellas carries the thoughts of intimacy and filtered light, and the notion of a 'water house' to the outside."

The bathhouse is situated in the historic center of Salzburg, continuing on the one side the late 19th century perimetral buildings of Auerspergstrasse, and opening to the greenery of the Kurgarten, next to the Mirabell Palace, on the other side. The six-story building houses spa and rehabilitative treatments (including physiotherapy, gymnastics and electrotherapy) on the lower floors. From there a central, wide staircase leads to the twenty-five-meter-long sports pool, a four-meter-deep diving pool, tube slides and children's pools on the third floor; continuing to the sauna area and infinity pool on the top of the roof. Clad on the outside in white ceramic vertical blinds, not unlike Le Corbusier's famous brise-soleils, their rhythm is interrupted on the third-floor level, where the curving, panoramic window provides views to the surrounding park and city for the pool visitors. Indoors, similar white ceramic modular tiles cover the large-scale, undulating ceiling that culminates in a magnificent, circular light well that extends to the roof through two floors. Making use of the parametric architectural language of today, the space refers also to the typology of modernist swimming pools—through its uninterrupted span of the ceiling and the natural skylight that remains hidden at first—interpreting it through contemporary materials and structural means.

Remaining invisible to the users, the wide span of the pool is held up by a complex construction using large steel struts in combination with concrete slabs.

The municipally-owned Paracelsus Bad & Kurhaus, named after a 16th-century doctor who lived in Salzburg shortly before his death, and whose statue stands in the Kurgarten park, has existed on this spot already since 1956. The new bathhouse was erected on the site in 2019, taking into account changed demands on sustainability, energy efficiency and circulation. This includes a set of high-tech solutions that help to recycle residual heat and air in the building or use ventilation for optimal climate conditions indoors. But also the vertical ceramic "sunbreakers" that envelop the building play their role, avoiding overheating in the summer months. (ak)

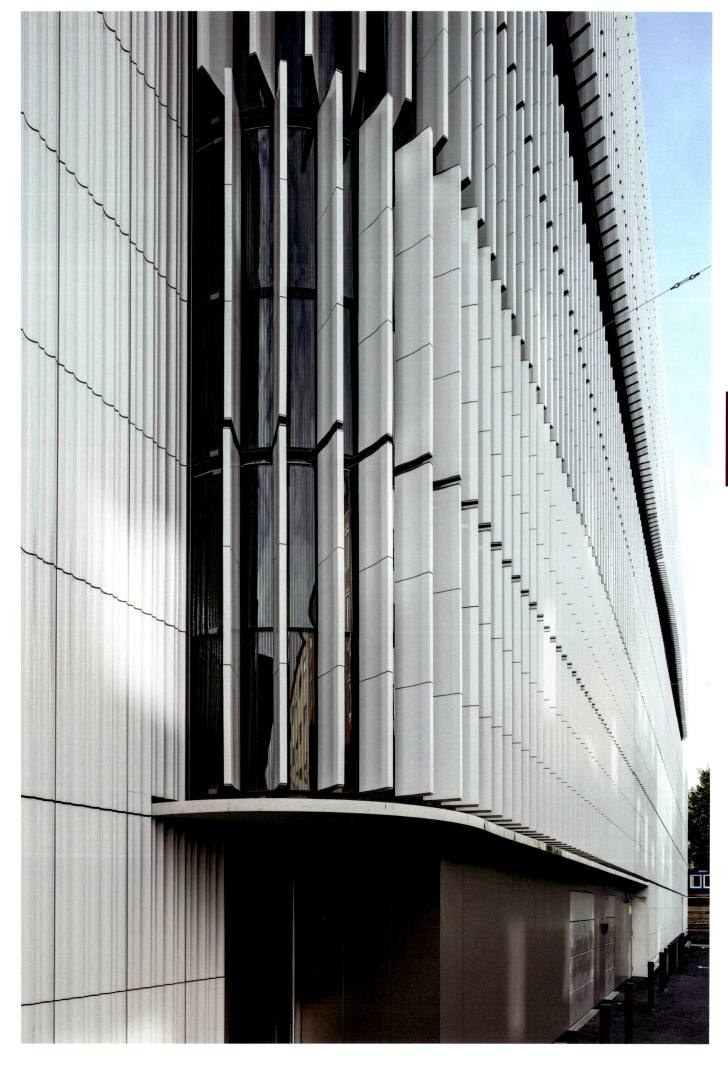

Paracelsus Bad & Kurhaus

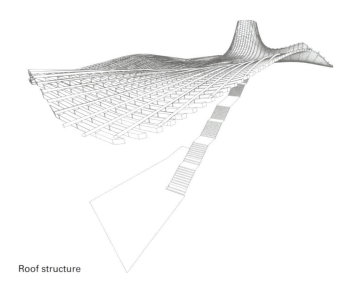

Roof structure

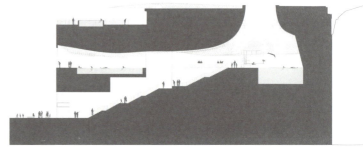

Section

The swimming area on the 3rd floor is completely glazed.

View from the sauna area to the Mülln parish church

WALLMAKERS
Pirouette House

Vinu Daniel

ARCHITECT/S
WALLMAKERS,
Ernakulam,
Kerala/India

LOCATION
Thiruvananthapuram,
Kerala, India

BUILDING PURPOSE
Single-family housing

CONSTRUCTION PERIOD
2018–2020

BRICK TYPE
Brick veneer,
clay blocks

The Pirouette House is situated in an urban area in Thiruvananthapuram, the capital of the state of Kerala in South India, and is surrounded on all four sides by residential buildings. Its regular two-story volume of concrete horizontal floors and beams is partitioned by diagonally slanting walls of red brick, producing room configurations that are flowing and undulating in several directions. A bedroom that starts to morph into a honeycomb structure, an informal living room where the oblique wall looks like part of an old fortification, the main entrance, above which walls touch each other as if in passing. As in a pirouette of a dancer, the brick surfaces seem to move by turning around their axis, with the upper rim racing ahead and the lower one lagging behind. The effect, however, is not solely formal or emotional; the slanting forms direct air flows through the house and provides shade in the tropical climate. Their position was carefully choreographed to create larger interconnected spaces that allow for withdrawal and privacy at the same time.

The red brick walls were laid in a rat-trap bond, in which the bricks placed on their edges were pushed out of the plane of the wall. This allows material to be saved but also produces a hollow space within the wall that insulates the interiors from heat and allows service infrastructure to be concealed. Adding a decorative twist to the wall, the architects have placed two transversal bricks in the bond end to end, so that a quarter of the brick sticks out from the wall surface, resulting in sculptural and optical variability. The rat trap bond is an homage to the British-born Indian architect Laurie Baker, who spent his life in Kerala and developed ways to build houses that would be energy-efficient, use passive cooling methods, and simultaneously represent local craftsmanship and building techniques. He advocated the bond as a way to reduce building costs but also allow for plasticity that increased the strength of the constructions. The principles of sustainability are likewise reflected by the re-use of the scaffolding pipes from the construction stage in the central staircase and the grillwork, and the recycling of the wooden scaffolding planks as part of the flooring in the living areas.

"The Pirouette House features the 'Last of the Mohicans' fired bricks as an ode to the stellar practice of Laurie Baker with spaces that are made beautiful by the pure geometry and patterns created by the walls that seem to be coming alive and pirouetting around."

This approach to inventive re-use represents the broader ethos of the architectural collective Wallmakers, who focus in their work on natural materials and on what traditionally has been called waste. Out of these components the architects produce details that are functional and evocative, putting into question the traditional separation between utilitarian and aesthetic materials. The use of local handcrafted bricks further aims to promote local traditional brick kilns that have been marginalized by the machine-made bricks. Redefining the building process in this way, the Pirouette House deals with many burning questions of the moment: How can architecture rely on local traditions and take into account the new changing climate reality? How can we maintain the comforts of modern living under these circumstances and do so in a sustainable way? [ak]

Building outside the box

251

Pirouette House

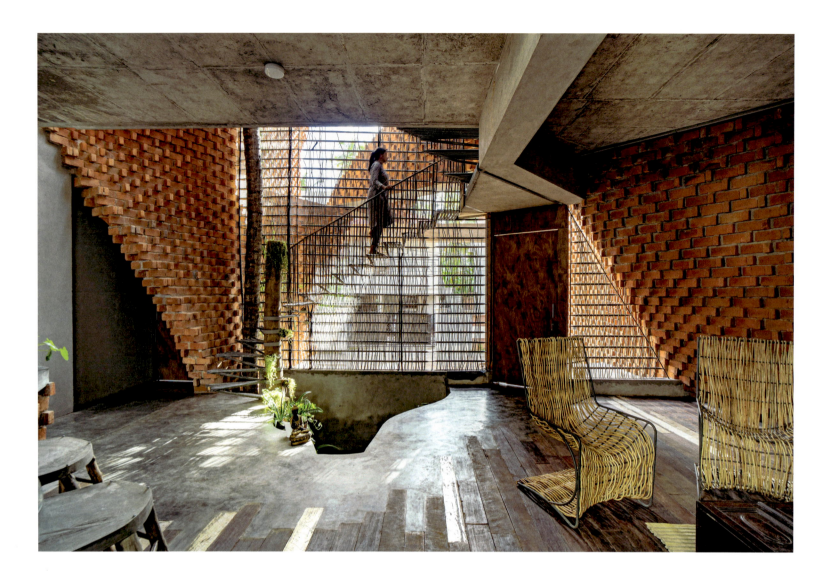

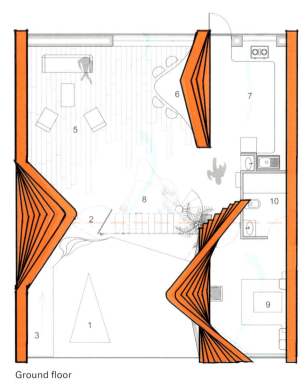

Ground floor

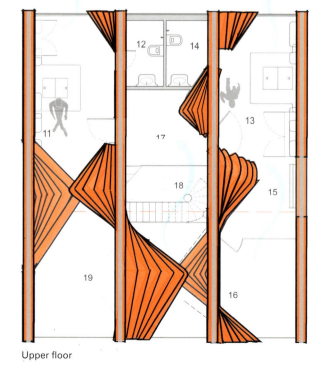

Upper floor

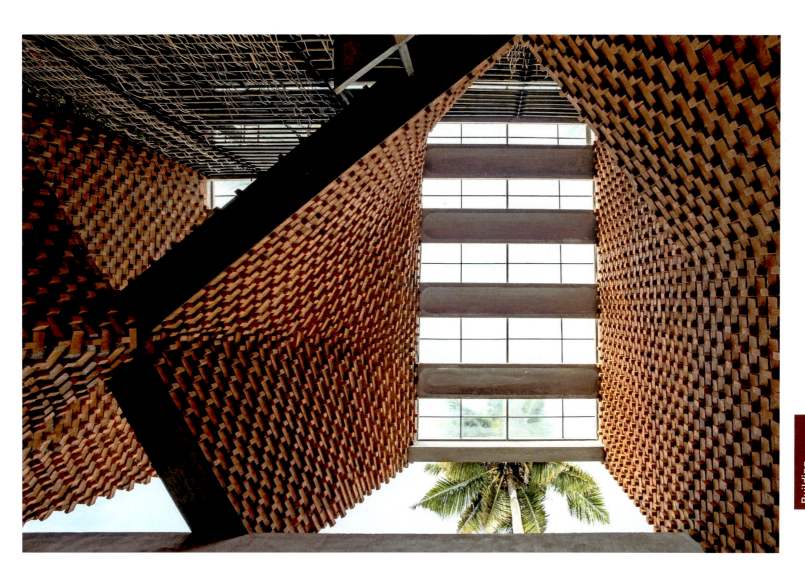

Building outside the box

BODENSTEINER FEST ARCHITECTS
Casa Rossa Chemnitz

Annette Fest and Christian Bodensteiner

ARCHITECT/S
bodensteiner fest Architects BDA Urban Planners PartGmbB, Munich/Germany

LOCATION
Chemnitz, Germany

BUILDING PURPOSE
Apartment housing

CONSTRUCTION PERIOD
2018–2020

BRICK TYPE
Original bricks from 1910, facing bricks

In new buildings, it may no longer be very suitable for new aesthetic experiences — when dealing with existing buildings, the dictum "less is more" is one that leads to inspiring results. The architects Annette Fest and Christian Bodensteiner demonstrated this impressively in Chemnitz. The building at Giesserstrasse 41 was empty for 30 years. Shortly after reunification, it shared this fate with many other houses here in the Sonnenberg neighborhood, a Gründerzeit-era district close to the train station and the city center. Gradually the quarter rose in popularity again, the houses were renovated, but this one building continued to deteriorate. It had to be foreclosed — an opportunity that the architects seized.

It was high time: The wooden ceilings had already collapsed, the roof was leaking, and not much of the red plaster on the bricks that gave the project its name could be seen. Today, however, the house is no longer red, because the façade bricks, still those from 1910, were not re-plastered after cleaning, but merely re-grouted, coated with a light mineral glaze and hydrophobized, so that the traces of processing and the time could expressively be turned into a "flair of the imperfect" — the plasticity of the façade vigorously emerges as a result. Concrete lintels, cornices and steel girders were restored, broad edging covers the window frames to the point that only their dark red-lacquered opening sashes appear.

> "Casa Rossa tells of the universality of bricks as building material: Freed from plaster after a hundred years, something new arises."

The interior is also characterized by a slimmed-down aesthetic based on the materiality of the existing building. Remnants of plaster were removed, bringing out the brick walls even more. New brick ceilings replace the ramshackle ones made of wood and improve the sound insulation. The attic was removed and the bricks were used to repair damage to the existing walls on the floors below and in the stairwell and to put in new walls. A new roof raised towards the courtyard made it possible to set up a maisonette apartment. The five apartments on the floors below also have their individual character: All the salvaged room doors were restored and installed in one apartment on the first floor. In the apartment on the third floor, the living area is a "brick loft" with exposed masonry. Wooden floors, as well as concrete, brick and steel surfaces, were treated solely with glazes and oil, thus allowing their materiality to remain experienceable; the white new doors and fixtures make them stand out all the more clearly.

High insulation thicknesses and an energy concept supported by solar thermal systems ensure that the house is not inferior to a new building in terms of its energy parameters. The combination of respectfully preserved building fabric and reduced material aesthetics is only possible in a house with such a history. [ch]

Casa Rossa Chemnitz

After one hundred years, the house presents itself for the first time with an unplastered brick façade.

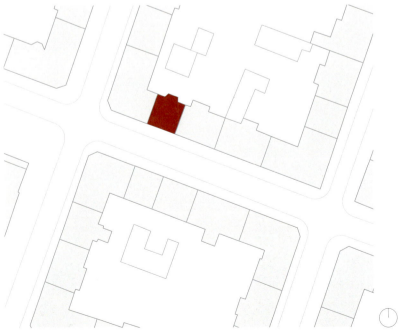

Site plan

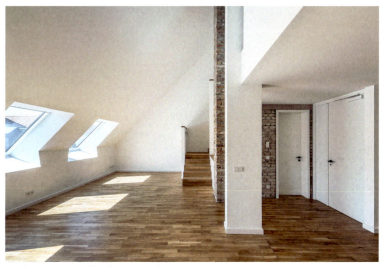 

Inside, too, selected walls were stripped of plaster.

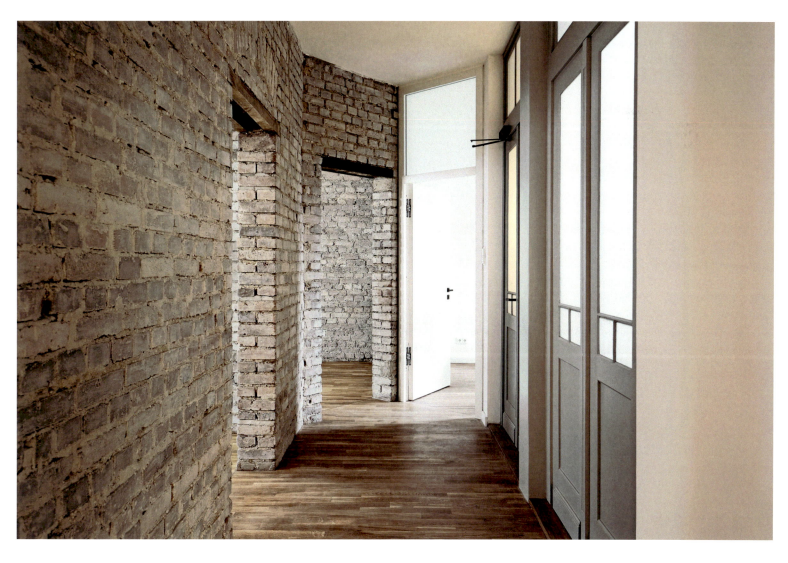

BANGKOK PROJECT STUDIO
The Elephant World : Non-Human-Centered Architecture

Boonserm Premthada

ARCHITECT/S
Bangkok Project Studio, Bangkok/Thailand

LOCATION
Ta Klang Village, Thailand

BUILDING PURPOSE
Culture

CONSTRUCTION PERIOD
2018–2020

BRICK TYPE
Clay blocks, facing bricks, roof tiles

The Elephant World in Ta Klang Village, in Eastern Thailand, is a space for interaction between animals and humans. Elephants have a unique status in Thailand, especially among the Kui people, where they are seen as part of the family structure and live close to their custodians. The center in the country's oldest elephant village—a place where elephants and humans live together—is dedicated to investigating and representing this interaction. Funded by the government to preserve the unique culture and the existing animal species, it is composed of three sections: the elephant museum, an observation tower and an arena for events and celebrations. Together these buildings form a site where nature and culture can come together, contributing to the exceptional genre of architecture for animals.

> "We learn to be human through the architecture, animals and nature."

The museum building consists of a system of red-brick walls that rise gradually from the ground to form a labyrinth-like building with exhibition areas, a library, a seminar room and a cafeteria that are interconnected by open-air paths. Running between the sturdy, uncovered walls, the paths are also wide enough for elephants to move through them. The partitions between different closed spaces, on the other hand, are of glass, undoing the strict separation of the inside and outside and allowing the exhibitions and activities to seamlessly extend to the outdoor areas. To the west of the museum is a large arena for cultural events and religious ceremonies, the Cultural Courtyard, which is surrounded by a low mound used for seating and is covered by a gable roof on concrete posts. The mounds are made of the soil from a newly dug rainwater reservoir to collect water for elephants. The loose soil under the canopy seating can be used by the animals for cooling their bodies and scaring off insects. The 28-meter-high observation tower to the south of the arena marks the entrance to the whole complex and provides spectacular views over the territories. It has an outer latticed brick shell with a steel staircase inside from where the alternating pattern of the bricks provides a diversity of views for the visitors on their way to the top. The upper platform is surrounded by brick posts with different heights, creating a metaphor for the building as if disappearing into air. The large quantity of bricks used for the buildings were made from local clay, using the craftsmen and technique specific to the region. In this way the construction process provided jobs for locals and gave new value to the traditional building material.

The Elephant World belongs to a unique architectural typology that sees its primary users to be animals rather than humans. If this kind of building can mostly be found in zoos (one could think here of the famous penguin pool in London Zoo by Berthold Lubetkin), then here the structure is part of an existing village and represents its daily life. Before embarking on the project, the architects conducted research in the area on the life patterns of its inhabitants and studied the structures that were made especially for the elephants. The large walkways of the museum, the massing of its walls, the scale of the arena and the bulky concrete posts carrying the canopy wall—all these details reflect the new functionality that derives from the needs of its users. [ak]

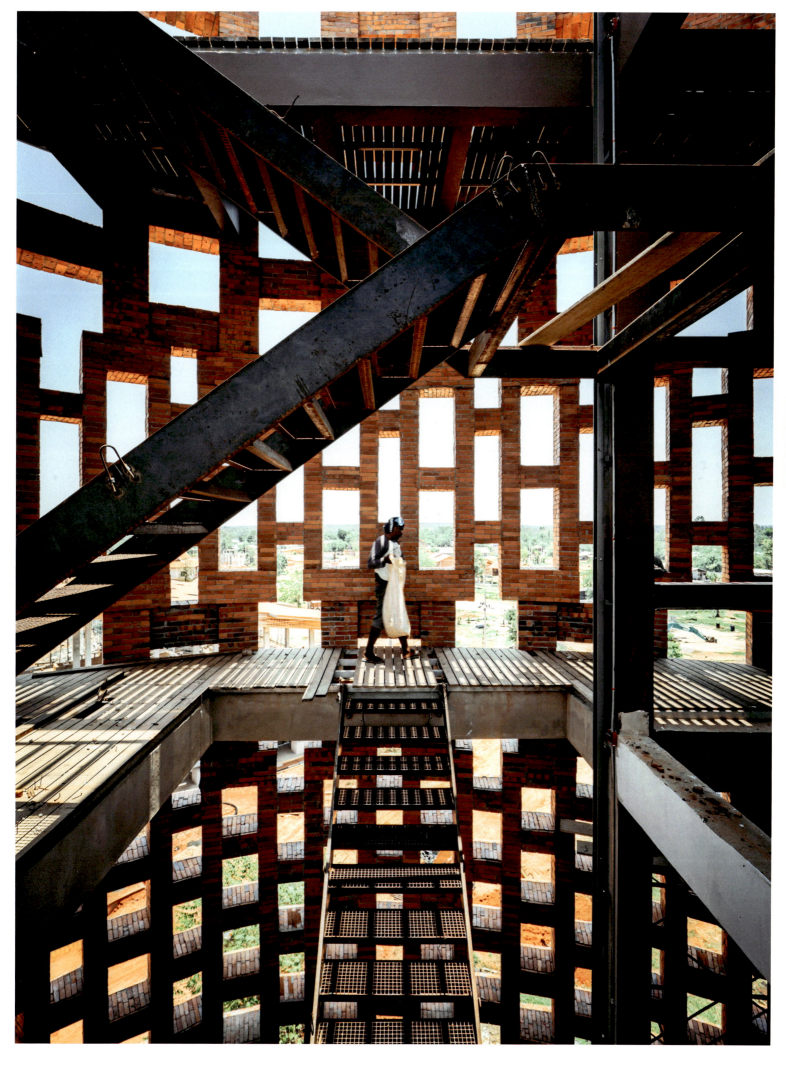

Building outside the box

The Elephant World : Non-Human-Centered Architecture

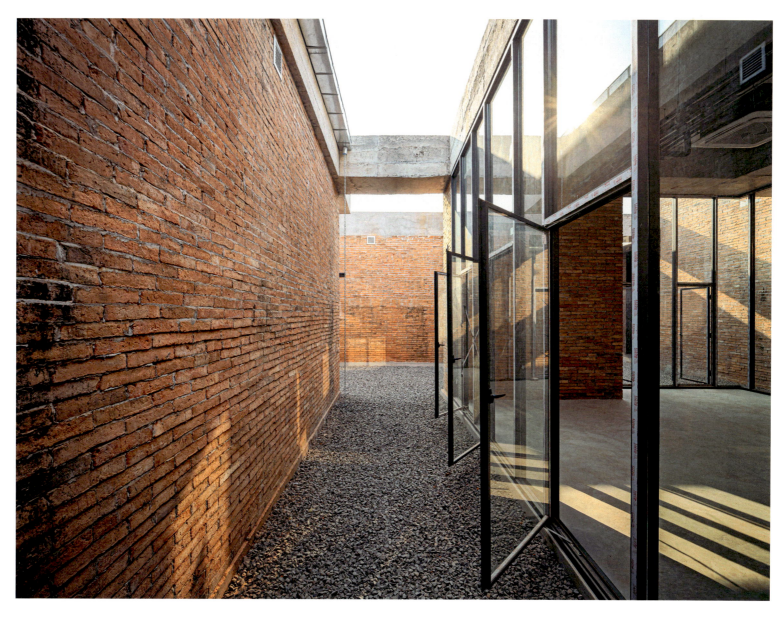

HARQUITECTES
Clos Pachem Winery

Xavier Ros, Josep Ricart, Roger Tudó and David Lorente

ARCHITECT/S
Harquitectes,
Sabadell/Spain

LOCATION
Gratallops, Tarragona,
Spain

BUILDING PURPOSE
Winery

CONSTRUCTION PERIOD
2017–2019

BRICK TYPE
Roof tiles,
paving bricks,
clay blocks

It sounds like a simple task: a new winery was to be designed for a winemaker in a Catalonian mountain village. But it wasn't that simple after all: Because the property in the middle of the narrow buildings directly below the church that crowns the location required a sensitive approach. And as if that weren't demanding enough, the architects from Harquitectes also accepted the challenge of using architectural means to guarantee stable temperature and humidity conditions required for the winery.

"Interaction on another scale."

They designed a two-part complex. At the edge of the irregular property, aligned with the alley, the actual winery for the production and storage of the wine was constructed as a simple cuboid. In order to integrate it into the surroundings, the brick façade was grouted with lime mortar. The space between the winery and the church hill, as well as the adjacent structures, was used for a high passage, which opens onto the site with a loggia: This is where visitors and grapes are received, wine is sold, and tastings take place. Walls and floors feature red, untreated brick and glimpses of the cellar can be caught on different levels. Flat roofs at different heights were arranged in such a way that different spatial dimensions result, but above all that the rainwater can collect on them, run from one roof to the other, and thus cool the air before it flows away.

Above the cellar with the storage room, the temperature and humidity of which remains constant thanks to the open ground, is the hall, flanked by adjoining rooms where the grape juice ferments. The high, three-story space ensures that the warm layers of air do not reach the barrels. The reinforced brick ceiling helps keep the indoor climate stable, because perforated bricks are laid vertically in its upper area to enable the air to circulate through the gaps. Walls up to 1.75 meters thick and consisting of layers of reinforced brick slabs are integrated into this system. On the one hand, they form an outwardly insulating shell; on the other hand, they are erected over pillars so that the air between them can escape downwards. In addition, a heat exchange system was integrated above the ceiling. It uses the high storage capacity of the water through a closed loop during the day to cool the air that is directed into the room via the ceiling and walls; at night, the heat absorbed by the water during the day can be dissipated again through the roof. A second loop uses the ground to cool the interior.

The proportions and a long common tradition could tempt one to consider the proximity of the winery and church to be very plausible. In any case, architecturally they complement each other wonderfully. [ch]

> "The challenge was to allow the winery itself to contribute to the biodynamic winemaking process."

Building outside the box

Clos Pachem Winery

Site plan

A passage flanks the heart of the wine production.

Vistas in all directions are provided.

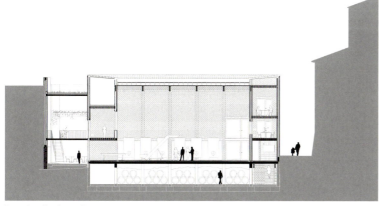
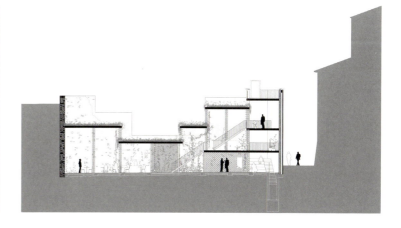

Longitudinal sections

CTA | CREATIVE ARCHITECTS
Wall House

Bui The Long

ARCHITECT/S
CTA | Creative Architects, Ho Chi Minh City / Vietnam

LOCATION
Bien Hoa, Vietnam

BUILDING PURPOSE
Single-family housing

CONSTRUCTION PERIOD
2018

BRICK TYPE
Clay blocks, facing bricks, ceramic panels, paving bricks

The name of this house in Bien Hoa, in the south of Vietnam, arouses the expectation that this is a closed, introverted building. That's right — but also precisely not. A wall encloses all functional areas — but at the same time it is an open, permeable structure that contributes to healthy and clean air inside.

> "The 'breathing shell' determines the appearance and volume of the outer house."

When designing the house for a three-generation family, two conceptual thoughts were guiding. The first is the house-in-house. Four smaller, two-story "houses" are placed in a large cubic form, which "presses" through the skin of the outer house in some spots, making the structure of the building also legible from the outside and not appearing as too introverted and closed. Inside they are grouped around a common center. This middle is partly two-story, with a gallery that distinguishes the common spaces as open and somewhat more intimate ones — spaces for dining together, the living area on the ground floor and the learning and playing area on the upper floor. The bedrooms, the kitchen and a study are situated in the inner houses. A nuanced gradation of areas for everyone emerges at one end of the scale and for individuals at the other end. This concept also makes it possible, apart from the stairs, to do without access areas such as corridors.

The second basic thought is that of the "breathing" shell, which determines the appearance and volume of the outer house. This shell is made of dark, defectively fired, perforated bricks, which, however, are not laid in the usual direction, but have been rotated by 90 degrees so that the air can circulate through their tubes, which run horizontally to the wall level. The idea behind this is not only to create a pleasant atmosphere inside with a continuous flow of air, but the bricks also serve a cleaning purpose, as the rough surfaces in the tubes remove coarse dirt particles from the air. Generous planting on the outer shell intensifies this cleaning effect. This turns the common spaces into a garden reminiscent of the one originally located on the property near the Dong Hai River.

The design of the wall from the simplest and most inexpensive basic material takes up the thought of breathing: In a moving and differently dense arrangement, the impression is created that the wall can actually breathe. It gives the conceptually strict notion a lightness that ideally complements the plants. Not only does the interaction provide for fresh and clean air at all times of the day and night — windows and skylights also ensure adequate natural lighting. Ultimately, the building is not only inexpensive due to the choice of material, but also in terms of maintenance: Fans and air conditioning systems can almost entirely be dispensed with. [ch]

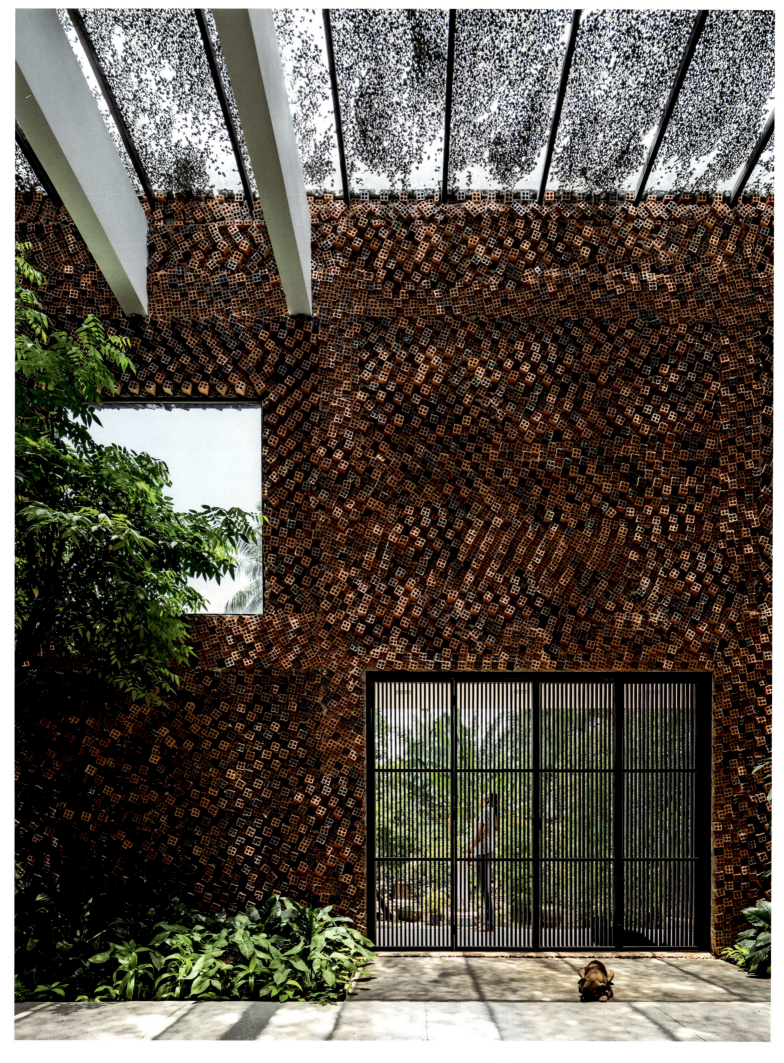

Building outside the box

Wall House

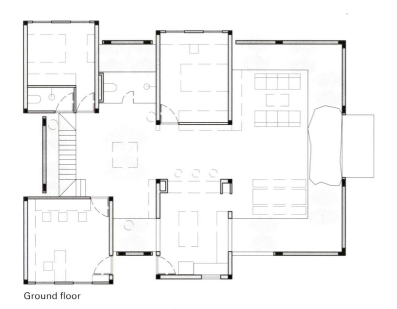
Ground floor

Upper floor

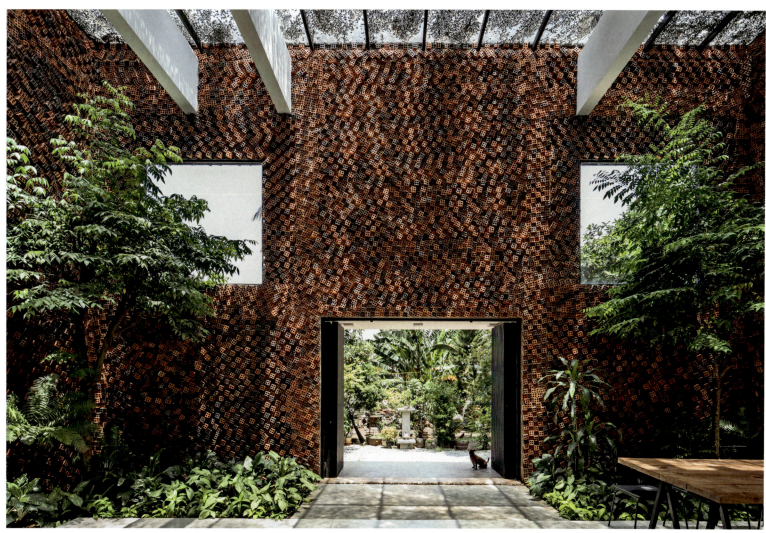

Air can flow through the tubes of the perforated bricks.

Building outside the box

269

MONADNOCK & DE ZWARTE HOND
Park Pavilion

Job Floris and Sandor Naus (Monadnock), Willem Hein Schenk (De Zwarte Hond)

ARCHITECT/S
Monadnock, Rotterdam, & De Zwarte Hond, Haarlem/ The Netherlands

LOCATION
Otterlo, The Netherlands

BUILDING PURPOSE
Culture

CONSTRUCTION PERIOD
2017–2019

BRICK TYPE
Facing bricks, paving bricks

De Hoge Veluwe is a 5,400-hectare-large national park in The Netherlands. In the middle of the landscape of heather, dunes and pines lies the Kröller-Müller Museum with one of the most important Van Gogh collections, numerous other works of early modernism and a large sculpture garden. The park also has a lot to offer architecturally, including the museum building by Henry van de Velde and Wim Quist, a hunting lodge designed by Hendrik Petrus Berlage, as well as four entrance pavilions by MVRDV.

Now there is a new visitor pavilion in the heart of the park as well, replacing a rather simple, barn-like structure with a self-service restaurant. The new pavilion sees itself as a modern interpretation of a country house and aims to interact with the landscape.

The silhouette of the asymmetrical, double roof catches the eye from afar. If one approaches the building from the parking lot, one first sees the west façade clad with vertical slats. The main entrance is around the corner in the gently curved south façade. There the eaves height is very low, lending the access area an intimate vibrancy.

A visitor information center with a shop and a restaurant occupies the ground floor. With its barrel vault, wood-paneled walls and turquoise-tiled fireplace, the design of which is clearly influenced by Berlage's Art Deco style, the central space looks like a large living room. On the south side, it opens to the dune landscape via a folded glass façade, creating seating niches both inside and outside.

"The bricks provide for a robust embracement, thereby confirming the idea of a welcoming space for visitors and making them feel comfortable and accommodated. The rich, nuanced color tones connect with the sand tones of the adjacent landscape."

On the contrary, the other side of the pavilion is much more closed. The vertical rib motif returns, but now above a brick plinth. A sculptural spiral staircase leads from the ground floor to the first floor, where event spaces can be found. They border on a communal balcony with a bricked parapet, which hides the delivery area below from view.

The light color palette of the pavilion refers to the sandy soil and dunes. Champagne-colored, anodized aluminum defines the image on three sides. It is combined with beige-colored, partially sintered waterstruck bricks with reddish and rose-colored accents. The brick was grouted flat to emphasize the surface of the outer walls more than the individual bricks.

The building thrives on the contrast between zigzag shapes and curves, between earthy brick and shiny aluminum, but also between abstraction and homeyness. The historical references—Dutch country houses, barns and the architecture of Berlage—are clearly recognizable but cast in modern forms. At the same time, the double roof turns the pavilion into a landmark and makes it stand out in the forest and heather landscape. It thus knows how to assert itself well between the other architectural highlights in the national park. [ab]

Park Pavilion

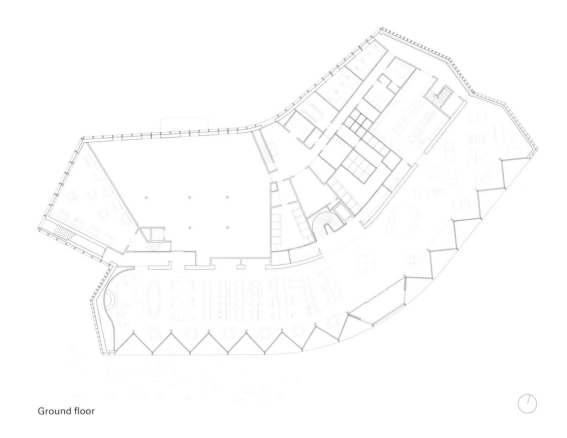

Ground floor

Building outside the box

The Authors

MATEVŽ ČELIK is an architect, writer, editor, researcher and developer of new cultural models in the fields of architecture and design. He is the founder and program director of the Future Architecture Platform, a pan-European platform for exchange and networking between architectural institutions and emerging talents. Until 2020 he was director of MAO, the Museum of Architecture and Design in Ljubljana, which under his leadership grew into a flagship national institution with international reach. Matevž Čelik stands behind the repositioning of BIO Ljubljana, the oldest design biennial in Europe, which has been transformed from a standard design exhibition into a live experiment to explore the potentials of design to instigate positive change. In 2016, 2018 and 2020, Matevž Čelik served as the Commissioner of the Slovenian Pavilion at La Biennale di Venezia. He is a member of the advisory board of the Archipelago festival in Geneva.

ANNA CYMER, architecture historian, graduated from the University of Warsaw in art history, works as a journalist focused on promoting knowledge about architecture; writes about contemporary architecture for popular and specialized media; laureate of the National Chamber of Polish Architects journalism award, author of the book *Architecture in Poland 1945–1989*.

WOJCIECH CZAJA, born in Ruda Śląska (Poland) in 1978, studied architecture at the Vienna University of Technology. He works as a journalist, author and moderator for *Der Standard* and *db deutsche bauzeitung*, among others. His main topics are architecture, urban culture and real estate management. He is a lecturer at the University of Art and Design in Linz and at the University of Applied Arts in Vienna. In addition, he is a member of the urban development advisory board of the Lower Austrian municipality of Waidhofen/Ybbs. His book publications include *Das Buch vom Land* (2015), *motion mobility* (2017, with Matthias Boeckl), *Hektopolis. Ein Reiseführer in hundert Städte* (2018) and *Frauen Bauen Stadt* (2021, with Katja Schechtner). During the Corona lockdown of 2020 he started his photo project *Almost*. This resulted in a book series and a touring exhibition that has already been shown at the Wien Museum, at the WIR SIND WIEN festival, as well as in Kraków, Zagreb and Vukovar.

ISABELLA LEBER

After graduating from high school Isabella Leber studied music—violoncello in Grenoble, France. In 1990 she began her architecture studies in Karlsruhe, which she continued in London, where she acquired her first diploma, the RIBA Part 2. In 1998 she received a second diploma in Karlsruhe, with a focus on urban planning. After several years abroad in Denmark, she returned to her hometown Munich, where she initially worked as a freelance architect, mainly in existing buildings. In 2011 she founded Pool Leber Architects with Martin Pool. In addition to experimenting with new building materials such as lightweight concrete and vacuum insulation, dealing with and maintaining existing buildings is an important part of the office's architectural portfolio. After teaching positions in the architectural heritage course and a guest professorship for building theory at Augsburg University, in 2020 she became Professor for Building with Existing Structures and Design at Wiesbaden University.

HENRIETTA PALMER is an architect and researcher with a focus on urban planning and sustainability. She has also held various teaching positions. She was Artistic Professor of Urban Design at Chalmers University of Technology in Gothenburg, Sweden, in parallel with being Deputy Scientific Director at Mistra Urban Futures from 2015 to 2019. From 2005 to 2015 she was Professor of Architecture at the Royal Institute of Art (KKH), Stockholm, where she designed and conducted the transdisciplinary post-master's programme *Resources*, engaging in urban challenges with contextual studies across a number of cities globally. Her research concerns just urban transformation processes stemming from social-spatial practices. For example, she sees the urgency in understanding migration at the core of urban processes. Henrietta has also an engagement in pedagogical and research methodologies, especially for transdisciplinary research and for transformative learning.

Pre-Jury/Authors Project Texts

ANNEKE BOKERN, born in Frankfurt, Germany, is an architecture journalist and owner of architectural guiding company architour in Amsterdam. She holds an M.A. in Art History from the Freie Universität Berlin and has been living in Amsterdam since 2000. Her publications focus on Dutch architecture and design. Her articles have been published in various German and international magazines, including *Bauwelt, Baumeister, Domus, Topos* and *uncube magazine*. She also contributes to book publications and has published an architecture guide to Rotterdam. With her company architour she organizes architecture tours for groups in the Netherlands.

CHRISTIAN HOLL studied architecture in Aachen, Florence and Stuttgart. From 1997 to 2004 he was the editor of *db – deutsche bauzeitung*, and founded frei04 publizistik together with Ursula Baus and Claudia Siegele in 2004, where he published reports, commentaries and essays from 2014 to 2016. Since 2017 frei04 publizistik has been the publisher of the magazine for architecture and urbanism *marlowes.de*. Holl is a book author, works as a freelance editor, journalist and critic, and had teaching assignments in Darmstadt, Stuttgart, Wuppertal, Kaiserslautern and Frankfurt on Main. From 2005 to 2010 he was a scientific assistant at the Urban Design Institute of the University of Stuttgart, from 2007 to 2013 editor of *germanarchitects.com*. Since 2008 he has been a curator and member of the exhibition committee of the "architekturgalerie am weißenhof," since 2010 managing director of the Association of German Architects Hessen (BDA Hessen).

ANDRES KURG is professor of architectural history and theory at the Institute of Art History, Estonian Academy of Arts in Tallinn. His academic work specializes in the art and architecture of the Baltic countries and Russia during the Soviet era, with a special focus on the influence of technological transformations and changes in everyday life to the built environment from the 1960s to the1980s. He has published articles in *AA Files, ARTMargins, the Journal of Architecture* and *Home Cultures*, and contributed to several collected volumes and exhibition catalogues. He has curated exhibitions on Soviet architecture and design, including *Centrifugal Tendencies: Tallinn, Moscow, Novosibirsk* at the Museum for Architectural Drawing in Berlin (2017), and held guest fellowships at the Getty Research Institute and Yale University.

The Jury

JESPER GOTTLIEB received his formal training at University of California, Berkeley, and at The Royal Danish Academy of Fine Arts, where he graduated with a master's degree in architecture in 1983.

Until 1993, when he became partner in Gottlieb Paludan Architects, he worked with various architectural firms in both the US and Denmark, and over the years he has taught at schools of architecture in California, New Mexico and Copenhagen.

Jesper Gottlieb has been the creative director of Gottlieb Paludan Architects for almost three decades and has won national and international recognition and awards for his contribution to industrial and infrastructural architecture with winning the Brick Award 20 in the category Working together for the City Archive in Delft.

TINA GREGORIČ was born in Slovenia, where she studied at the Faculty of Architecture of the University of Ljubljana. She finished her postgraduate studies with distinction in 2002 at the Architectural Association in London. Since then, she has worked with Zaha Hadid Architects in London, taught at the AA and the TU Graz. In 2003 she founded Dekleva Gregorič Architects together with her partner Aljoša Dekleva in Ljubljana. In 2014 she became professor of architecture and head of department at TU Wien.

The work of Dekleva Gregorič Architects pursues the concepts of "research by design" and "design by research." With this approach, the office has been nominated for the Mies van der Rohe Award several times and received the Wan House of the Year 2015 Award and the International Architecture Award 2012, just to name a few.

Their most well-known projects include the University Campus Livade 1.0 in Izola, Slovenia, "XXS House" in Ljubljana, and the "Clifftop House" in Maui, Hawaii.

INGRID VAN DER HEIJDEN discovered after a career in marketing and a professional training as a cabinetmaker, that she has the spatial skills to find her way in architecture.

She co-founded Civic, an internationally operating firm for public architecture, established in 2015 by four architects and working from Amsterdam. They design libraries, bridges, cultural buildings, town halls, squares, educational and residential buildings, streets, sculptures and stations. Architecture is not an autonomous discipline for Civic, but a public task. Their designs anticipate the spatial, as well as social, cultural, economic and ecological contexts. Research plays a crucial role in their design process, and they develop variants at every stage.

Ingrid's work focuses on architectural form, sensoric qualities of materials and production processes. She studies the evolution of building types, materials and their context and experiment with its possibilities. She seeks a sustainable architecture that is just as interesting in 50 years as it is now: poetic pragmatism, timeless and pioneering.

WILFRIED KUEHN is a partner of the architecture bureau Kuehn Malvezzi, a curator and an author. Since 2018 he has been teaching spatial design and drafting at the Vienna University of Technology.

Kuehn Malvezzi conceive architecture as a cultural practice that addresses social and political relationships beyond typological categories. The office, founded in 2001, became internationally known for its redesign and expansion of numerous museum buildings. Over the past ten years, Kuehn Malvezzi has expanded its portfolio to include buildings on complex inner-city sites, residential construction, and designs on an urban scale.

Current projects include the new building for the Insectarium at the Botanical Gardens in Montreal and the interfaith House of One, an exposed brick structure built over the foundations of Berlin's earliest church.

Kuehn Malvezzi's work has been shown in various international exhibitions, including the 10th, 13th, and 14th Venice Architecture Biennales and the 1st and 2nd Chicago Architecture Biennials.

BRIGITTE SHIM was born in Kingston, Jamaica and completed her architectural and environmental studies at the University of Waterloo, Canada. In 1994, Shim and her partner A. Howard Sutcliffe founded Shim-Sutcliffe Architects in Toronto, Canada. Their design practice explores the integration and interrelated scales of architecture, landscape, furniture and fittings. Shim-Sutcliffe have realized built work in Canada, the United States, Russia and Asia focusing on place-making.

Professor Brigitte Shim has been a faculty member at the Daniels Faculty of Architecture, Landscape and Design at the University of Toronto since 1988. She was the 2019 Louis I. Kahn Professor of Architectural Design at Yale University's School of Architecture and has been a visiting chair and lecturer at Harvard University's Graduate School of Design, The Cooper Union, The University of Auckland, the École Polytechnique Fédérale de Lausanne and others.

Shim and Sutcliffe have received numerous awards, in 2013, Brigitte Shim they were awarded the Order of Canada, "for their contributions as architects designing sophisticated structures that represent the best of Canadian design to the world."

Imprint

Editor
Wienerberger AG

Editor-in-chief
Veronika Schuster-Hofinger

Copy editing
Eva Guttmann

Translation and proofreading
Brian Dorsey

Graphic design
Bruno Margreth, Aurelia Peter

Lithography, printing, and binding
DZA Druckerei zu Altenburg GmbH

© 2022 Park Books, Zurich

Park Books AG
Niederdorfstrasse 54
8001 Zurich
Switzerland
www.park-books.com

Park Books is being supported by the Federal Office of Culture with a general subsidy for the years 2021–2024.

All rights reserved; no part of this publication may be reproduced, stored in a retrieval system or transmitted in any form or by any means, electronic, mechanical, photocopying, recording, or otherwise, without the prior written consent of the publisher.

ISBN 978-3-03860-278-1

German edition:
Brick 22 – Ausgezeichnete internationale Ziegelarchitektur, 2022
ISBN 978-3-03860-277-4

Photo credits

Front cover: Spaceshift Studio

2–3: Dane Alonso
4–5: René Dürr
6–7: Karin Borghouts

10 left: Tim Van de Velde Photography
10 right: Schnepp Renou
11 left: René Dürr
11 middle: Studio Zhu Pei
11 right: Pedro Pegenaute
12: Uwe Strasser, Wienerberger AG
14: Daniel Hinterramskogler, Wienerberger AG

16–17: Luc Boegly
18–19: Spaceshift Studio
20–21: Simon Menges

FEELING AT HOME
26: Wojtek Affek / Bulletproof
29: Tim Van de Velde Photography
30: Vanelly Dumani
31–35, 37: José Fernando Gómez
38: OYO Architects
39–41: Tim Van de Velde Photography
42: ODDO architects
43–45: Hoang Le
46: McMahon Architecture
47–49: Fernando Manoso
50: Pia Riverola
51–53: Dane Alonso
54: Tanja Gabrijelčič
55–57: Miran Kambič
58: USE Studio
59–61: Ehsan Hajirasouliha – Mohammad Arab
62 left: Ineke Oostveen
62 right: Bureau SLA
63–65: Thijs Wolzak

LIVING TOGETHER
68: Filip Gorski
71: Sebastian van Damme
72: David Foessel
73–75, 77 top, 78, 79 top: Schnepp Renou
77 bottom: Simone Bossi
79 bottom: Avenier Cornejo
80: Danko Stjepanovic
81–83: Karin Borghouts
84: Wim Roefs
85–87: Réne de Wit, Breda
88: Andy Liffner
89–91: André Pihl / Wingårdhs
92: Dehullu Architecten
93–95: Dennis De Smet
96: Mangor & Nagel A/S
97, 98: Tom Jersø
99: Jens Lindhe
100: Casper Rila
101–103: Sebastian van Damme
104: Serge Anton
105–107: Stijn Bollaert & Maxence Dedry pour la cellule architecture
108–111: Caspar Sessler
112–115: Barbara Corsico
116: Sander Van de Weert
117–119: Stijn Bollaert
120–122 top: Orange Architects
122 bottom, 123 bottom: Ossip van Duivenbode
123 top: Frans Hanswijk

WORKING TOGETHER
126: Jože Suhadolnik
129: Parham Taghioff – Deed Studio
130: Baumschlager Eberle Architekten
131–135, 137: René Dürr
136: Max Carlo Kohal
138: VTN Architects
139–141 top: Hiroyuki Oki
141 bottom: VTN Architects
142, 144, 145 top: Hannu Rytky
143, 145 bottom: Mika Huisman
146: Gustavo Frittegotto
147–149: Manuel Cucurell
150: Peter Christensen / TRANSFORM
151, 153: Anders Sune
152: Rasmus Hjortshøj
154: Deed Studio
155–157: Parham Taghioff – Deed Studio
158: Jiaxi Yang & Zhu Zhe
159–161: Pedro Pegenaute
162–165: Tuomas Kivinen, Max Plunger

SHARING PUBLIC SPACES
168: Henrik Sandsjö
171: Eugeni Pons
172: Studio Zhu Pei
173–179: schranimage, Studio Zhu Pei
180: Jesús Arenas
181–183: Simon Menges
184: Simón Garcia
185–187: José Hevia, Simón Garcia
188 left: Klaas Verdu
188 right: Kevin Laloux
189–191: Stijn Bollaert
192: René Müller
193–195: Oliver Gerhartz
196: antonio virga architecte
197–199: Luc Boegly
200: Courtesy Colectivo C733
201–203: Rafael Gamo
204: Michel Slomka
205–207: Sergio Grazia
208: Daniel Salvador
209–211: Rubén P. Bescós
212 left: Ilse Liekens
212 right: Nada Mihajlović
213–215: Lucid
216: Zero Energy Design Lab
217–219: Andre Fanthome
220: umarchitekt
221–223: Gerhard Hagen
224: David Romero
225–227: Eugeni Pons

BUILDING OUTSIDE THE BOX
230: Florian Albert
233: Christian Richters
234: Jiaxi Yang & Zhu Zhe
235–241: Pedro Pegenaute
242: Gramazio Kohler Research, ETH Zurich
243–244, 245 top: Michael Lyrenmann
245 bottom: Gramazio Kohler Research, ETH Zurich
246: Philipp Horak
247–249: Christian Richters
250: Anand Jaju
251–253: Jino Sam
254: Florian Holzherr
255–257: Steffen Spitzner
258: IAMEVERYTHING.co
259–261: Spaceshift Studio
262: Harquitectes
263–264: Jesús Granada
265: Adrià Goula
266: CTA Creative Architects
267–269: Hiroyuki Oki
270 left: Bas Czerwinski
270 right: Rob Koenen
271–273: Stijn Bollaert

278–279: Thijs Wolzak
280–281: schranimage, Studio Zhu Pei
282–283: Hiroyuki Oki